剑桥
全真试题解析
CAMBRIDGE

IELTS 2

剑桥大学考试委员会　著

外 研 社 · 剑 桥
雅思考试培训教程

外语教学与研究出版社
剑桥大学出版社

(京)新登字 155 号

京权图字：01－2002－1489

图书在版编目(CIP)数据

剑桥雅思考试全真试题解析/剑桥大学考试委员会著.—北京：外语教学与研究出版社,2002.4
ISBN 7－5600－2682－6

Ⅰ.剑… Ⅱ.剑… Ⅲ.英语－高等学校－入学考试,国外－解题 Ⅳ.H319.6

中国版本图书馆 CIP 数据核字(2002)第 022894 号

Cambridge IELTS 2 by University of Cambridge Local Examinations Syndicate first published by Cambridge University Press 2000

This edition for the People's Republic of China is published by arrangement with The Press Syndicate of the University of Cambridge, Cambridge, United Kingdom.

外研社·剑桥雅思考试培训教程
剑桥雅思考试全真试题解析

剑桥大学考试委员会　著
*　　*　　*
项目管理：宋德伟
责任编辑：王　禹
出版发行：外语教学与研究出版社
社　　址：北京市西三环北路 19 号 (100089)
网　　址：http://www.fltrp.com
印　　刷：北京外国语大学印刷厂
开　　本：787×1092　1/16
印　　张：11
版　　次：2002 年 4 月第 1 版　2003 年 11 月第 3 次印刷
书　　号：ISBN 7－5600－2682－6/G·1268
定　　价：19.90 元
*　　*　　*
如有印刷、装订质量问题出版社负责调换
制售盗版必究　举报查实奖励 (010)68917826
版权保护办公室举报电话：(010)68917519

目　　录

Thanks and acknowledgements

We would like to thank the staff and students of the following institutions for their assistance in trialling these meterials:

Oxford Brookes University, University of Sunderland, Queen Mary & Westfield College, Cranfield University, UMIST, Glasgow University, University of Exeter, University of Nottingham, University of Salford, University of Sussex, Hilderstone College, South Bank University, University of Newcastle, ELT Banbury, University of Sheffield, Chichester Institute of Further Education, Lancaster University, University of Wolverhampton, Strathclyde University, Manchester Metropolitan University

The authors and publishers are grateful to the following for permission to reproduce copyright material. It has not always been possible to identify the sources of all the material used and in such cases the publishers would welcome information from the copyright owners.

The Economist for the extract on pp.14 – 15 from 'How to avoid that sinking feeling' © *The Economist*, London 4 Feb 1995; Harper Collins Publishers Ltd and Watson, Little Ltd for the extract on pp.23 – 4 from *Understanding Children's Minds by* Margaret Donaldson, Fontana Press 1987; Cambridge University Press for the extract on pp.42 – 3 from *The Cambridge Encyclopaedia of Language* by David Crystal, Cambridge University Press 1997; University of New South Wales Press for the extract on pp.47 – 8 from 'On the evolution of the port city' by Rhodes Murphies in *Brides of the Sea* ed. Frank Broeze, reproduced with permission of UNSW Press; *Understanding Global Issues* for the extract on pp.66 – 7 from 'The Motor Car: Preparing for the 21st Century', *Understanding Global Issues*, October 1995; Vince Beiser for the extract on pp.70 – 1 from *Macleans* magazine; *The Independent* for the extract on pp.83 – 4 form 'Green wave washes over mainstream shopping' by David Nicholson-Lord; *New Scientist* for the extract on pp.87 – 8; Faber and Faber Ltd for the extract on pp.91 – 2 from *Perilous Knowledge* by Tom Wilkie, Faber and Faber Ltd 1993; West Thames College for the extracts on pp.103 and 105; EF Education (www.ef.com) for the extract on p.119; Reader's Digest (Australia) for the listening material on pp.139 – 40.

The extract on pp.20 – 1 was taken from a research project by Paula Chapman, Queensland University of Technology; pp.106 – 7 form *The Pan Book of Astronomy* by James Muirden, Pan Books 1964; pp.121 – 2 from an article by Peter Wilson, *Sydney Morning Herald* 28.2.96.

Popperfoto for p.15; James Davis Worldwide for p.48; Telegraph Colour Library/VCL for p.103; NASA/ Genesis Space Photo Library for p.106; Jim Rice/Australian Financial Review for P.121.

Picture research by Sandie Huskinson-Rolfe of PHOTOSEEKERS
Design concept by Peter Ducker MSTD

Cover design by John Dunne

The cassettes which accompany this book were produced by Martin Williamson at Studio AVP, London.

前　言

雅思考试与《剑桥雅思考试全真试题解析》

IELTS（雅思）——国际英语水平测试——是由英国剑桥大学考试委员会（The University of Cambridge Local Examinations Syndicate—UCLES）、澳大利亚教育国际开发署（IDP Education Australia）及英国文化委员会（The British Council）联合开发的一种英语语言能力考试。目的是为准备进入以英语为主导教学语言的大学和学院进修的学生或以英语为母语的国家（目前指英联邦国家）移民人士测试英语水平而设。英国、澳大利亚、新西兰、加拿大、北美以及许多国家的众多院校均采用并认可这一语言测试系统。加拿大、澳大利亚、新西兰等国家的移民局均将这种考试成绩作为技术移民及其他类移民中衡量英语语言能力的唯一标准。

从 1980 年开始，雅思考试在全世界迅速发展，目前已经在 105 个国家设立了 224 个考点。中国大陆的北京、上海、成都、重庆、福州、广州、杭州、济南、南京、沈阳、深圳、天津、武汉、西安、厦门和大连等地都设有考点，每年都有数以万计的人员参加此项考试。

IELTS 考试包括两类：

培训类（General Training ）目前较多适用于移民

学术类（Academic）　　　　目前较多适用于留学

雅思考试全程时间 2 小时 55 分钟（包括听力的 10 分钟填写答题纸）。

一、听力部分（General Training 和 Academic 试卷一致）

通常考生会听到 4 段语音（独白部分及 2 人或多人对话部分）。共给 38－42 小题作答，考生将只听到（一次）语音，不会重复（边听边作答）此部分。所以考生作答时，千万别等待语音结束才作答（不要回头作答），考生可把答案先写在试卷上，30 分钟会话结束后，利用额外 10 分钟，再腾写在答题纸上。四段语音前两段中，内容以一般生活及社会状态、人际关系等不同情况模拟为主，后两段则针对具教育性、学术性、世界性的主题探讨，以对答（叙述）为主，但因其非常具有实际性、常识性，考生不必钻牛角尖。在会话进行中，边听边记录所听到的重点答案，记在问卷上（非答案卷），以免忘记或漏掉答案。

二、阅读部分（General Training 和 Academic 试卷不同）

Academic 类与 General Training 类的考题都以"三大段"的文章为基本结构，大约 1500－3000 字之间，内容多样，甚至有时以图示、表格的方式出现，考生答题的方式亦有多种形式，约38-42题。阅读部分的主题并不是为了考察学生对学术的专业度或认知度，所以学生千万别因对主题的陌生而紧张起来。A类与G类内容不同之处在于A类除生活化范畴之外，还加入考生在学业上、学术上的探讨与了解，而G类较着重于社会上的、语言的、工作训练等的主题。

三、写作部分（General Training 和 Academic 试卷第 1 单元不同，第 2 单元一致）

A类写作部分共 1 小时时间，分 2 大单元（Task 1 & Task 2）；Task 1 的考题通常以图片、表格座标、曲线图为基本形式，考生根据所给的资料，写出 150 个字以上的文章来叙述主题，组织并探讨主题，提出能支撑全文的论点。G类的 Task 1 考生以写一封信来应对考题中所给予的模拟状况或问题。A类与G类的 Task 2 非常相似，要求考生就考题的主题，用 250 字发表意见，通常考生可以从几种方式中选择其一来做为架构解决问题、表达自己的意见、支持或辩驳考题所给予的讯息。

四、口语部分（General Training 和 Academic 试卷一致）2001 年 7 月 1 日起进行了更新

10-15 分钟的一对一谈话（考生与主考官）。交谈主题非常口语化、生活化，轻松但也有一定的程序，交谈大致上分 4 小段（不是明显的区分，中间并无间断）：

第一段：会面，寒暄一番（约 1-2 分钟）。

第二段：主考官会鼓励（引导）考生多谈谈一般话题（生活作息、文化习惯、个人兴趣等等）（约 3-4 分钟），考生应勇敢发言。

第三段：主考官抽出一张角色扮演卡（Cue card），卡上写明一个模拟的事件，环境或状况，由考生向主考官依卡提出各种问题（约 3-4 分钟）。考生提出的问题须与卡上的主题相关，并可自由发挥。

第四段：主考官以询问考生个人有关（学业计划）或（未来展望）为主。A类与G类的考生因其考雅思的目的不同而不同。（约 34 分钟）（此段对答内容，是较多元化和深度化的，考生可以平时事先准备）。

雅思考试具有一套比较完备的出题、考试、评分系统和比较完备的题库系统。考题经过严格的审核和试测才进入题库。试题具有多样性，但材料又有大致相似的难度。虽然试题重复使用，但由于有足够的试题和不同的组合，试题只有小部分重合。雅思考试时间灵活，没有固定的时间，一般一个月一次，高峰季节一个月两次，特殊情况下，还可以获得 UCLES 授权自行组织考试。雅思考试的成绩为 9 分制，从 1-9 分的评估内容如下：

9 分	精通英语	成绩极佳，能将英语运用自如，精确、流利并能完全理解。
8 分	英语能力优秀	非常良好，能将英语运用自如，只是偶尔有间断和不恰当的用法，在不熟悉的状况下可能出现误解，可将复杂细节的争论掌握得相当好。
7 分	英语能力良好	良好，有能力运用英语，虽然有时在某些情况下会出现不准确、

不适当的用法和误解，但大致可将复杂的英语掌握得不错，也理解其全部内容。

6 分　英语能力能胜任　　及格，大致能有效地运用英语，虽然有不准确、不适当的用法和误解发生，但能使用并理解相当复杂的英语，特别是在对话题熟悉的情况下。（澳大利亚移民和英国留学分数线）

5 分　英语能力一般　　勉强及格，可部分运用英语，在大多数情况下可应付全部的意思，虽然可能犯下许多错误，但在本身领域内可掌握基本的沟通。（加拿大移民和新西兰移民分数线）

4 分　英语能力有限　　只限在熟悉的情况下基本上理解内容，在理解与表达上常发生问题，无法使用复杂英语。（英国预科分数线）

3 分　英语能力极有限　　在极熟悉的情况下，只能进行一般的沟通理解。

2 分　只能偶尔使用英语　　除非在熟悉的情况下，使用单词和简短的短句表达最基本的信息，在说写方面有重大的障碍。

1 分　不能使用英语　　不能通过，可能只能说几个单词，无法沟通。

《剑桥雅思考试全真试题解析》一书所收集的国际英语测试系统（雅思）训练资料由剑桥大学考试委员会提供，专门用于出版。本书向读者提供了一次绝佳的机会：通过对这些可靠资料的演练，读者可以熟悉雅思考试，锻炼应试技巧。

本书包含 4 套完整的学术类雅思考试试题，另外还附有针对一般类雅思考生的阅读和写作训练试题。本书向读者介绍了雅思考试的不同题型，并对剑桥大学考试委员会所采用的评分系统进行了解释说明。书后所附的综合答案和听力录音文本使本书非常适合学生部分或全部地使用本书资料用于自学。

本书磁带包含听力部分的录音资料，这些资料在时间安排上与考试完全一致。

外语教学与研究出版社

剑桥大学出版社

Introduction

The International English Language Testing System (IELTS) is widely recognised as a reliable means of assessing whether candidates are ready to study or train in the medium of English. IELTS is owned by three partners, The University of Cambridge Local Examinations Syndicate, the British Council and IDP Education Australia (through its subsidiary company IELTS Australia Pty Limited). The main purpose of this book of Practice Tests is to give future IELTS candidates an idea of whether their English is at the required level. Further information on IELTS can be found in the IELTS Handbook available free of charge from IELTS centres.

WHAT IS THE TEST FORMAT?

IELTS consists of six modules. All candidates take the same Listening and Speaking Modules. There is a choice of Reading and Writing Modules according to whether a candidate is taking the Academic or General Training version of the test.

Academic	General Training
For candidates taking the test for entry to undergraduate or postgraduate studies or for professional reasons	For candidates taking the test for entry to vocational or training programmes not at degree level, for admission to secondary schools and for immigration purposes

The test modules are taken in the following order.

Listening 4 sections, 40 items 30 minutes		
Academic Reading 3 sections, 40 items 60 minutes	OR	General Training Reading 3 sections, 40 items 60 minutes
Academic Writing 2 tasks 60 minutes	OR	General Training Writing 2 tasks 60 minutes
Speaking 10 to 15 minutes		
Total test time 2 hours 45 minutes		

Listening

This is in four sections, each with 10 questions. The first two sections are concerned with social needs. There is a conversation between two speakers and then a monologue. The final two sections are concerned with situations related to educational or training contexts. There is a conversation between up to four people and then a monologue.

A variety of question types is used, including: multiple choice, short-answer questions, sentence completion, notese/chart/table completion, labelling a diagram, classification, matching.

Candidates hear the recording once only and answer the questions as they listen. Ten minutes are allowed at the end to transfer answers to the answer sheet.

Academic Reading

There are three reading passages, of increasing difficulty, on topics of general interest and candidates have to answer 40 questions. The passages are taken from magazines, journals, books and newspapers. At least one text contains detailed logical argument.

A variety of question types is used, including: multiple choice, short-answer questions, sentence completion, notes/chart/table completion, labelling a diagram, classification, matching lists/phrases, choosing suitable paragraph headings from a list, identification of writer's views/attitudes—yes, no, not given.

General Training Reading

Candidates have to answer 40 questions. There are three sections of increasing difficulty, containing texts taken from notices, advertisements, leaflets, newspapers, instruction manuals, books and magazines. The first section contains texts relevant to basic linguistic survival in English, with tasks mainly concerned with providing factual information. The second section focuses on the training context and involves texts of more complex language. The third section involves reading more extended texts, with a more complex structure, but with the emphasis on descriptive and instructive rather than argumentative texts.

A variety of question types is used, including: multiple choice, short-answer questions, sentence completion, notes/chart/table completion, labelling a diagram, classification, matching lists/phrases, choosing suitable paragraph headings from a list, identification of writer's views/attitudes—yes, no, not given, or true, false, not given.

Academic Writing

There are two tasks and it is suggested that candidates spend about 20 minutes on Task 1, which requires them to write at least 150 words and 40 minutes on Task 2—250 words. The assessment of Task 2 carries more weight in marking than Task 1.

In Task 1 candidates are asked to look at a diagram or table and to present the information in their own words. They are assessed on their ability to organise, present and possibly compare data, describe the stages of a process, describe an object or event, explain how something works.

In Task 2 candidates are presented with a point of view, argument or problem. They are assessed on their ability to present a solution to the problem, present and justify an opinion, compare and contrast evidence and opinions, evaluate and challenge ideas, evidence or arguments.

Candidates are also judged on their ability to write in an appropriate style.

General Training Writing

There are two tasks and it is suggested that candidates spend about 20 minutes on Task 1, which requires them to write at least 150 words and 40 minutes on Task 2—250 words. The assessment of Task 2 carries more weight in marking than Task 1.

In Task 1 candidates are asked to respond to a given problem with a letter requesting information or explaining a situation. They are assessed on their ability to engage in personal correspondence, elicit and provide general factual information, express needs, wants, likes and dislikes, express opinions, complaints, etc.

In Task 2 candidates are presented with a point of view, argument or problem. They are assessed on their ability to provide general factual information, outline a problem and present a solution, present and justify an opinion, evaluate and challenge ideas, evidence or arguments.

Candidates are also judged on their ability to write in an appropriate style.

Speaking

This consists of a conversation between the candidate and an examiner and takes between 10 and 15 minutes. There are five sections:

1   Introduction
The examiner and candidate introduce themselves and the candidate is encouraged to talk briefly about their life, home, work and interests.
2   Extended discourse
The candidate is encouraged to speak at length about some familiar topics of general interest or of relevance to their culture, place of living or country of origin. This will involve explanation, description or narration.
3   Elicitation
The candidate is given a task card with some information on it and is encouraged to take the initiative and ask questions either to elicit information or to solve a problem.
4   Speculation and Attitudes
The candidate is encouraged to talk about their future plans and proposed course of study. Alternatively the examiner may choose to return to a topic raised earlier.
5   Conclusion
The interview is concluded.

Candidates are assessed on their ability to communicate effectively with native speakers of English. The assessment takes into account evidence of communicative strategies and appropriate use of grammar and vocabulary.

HOW IS IELTS SCORED?

IELTS results are reported on a nine-band scale. In addition to the score for overall language ability IELTS provides a score, in the form of a profile, for each of the four skills (Listening, Reading, Writing and Speaking). These scores are also reported on a nine-band scale. All scores are recorded on the Test Report Form along with details of the candidate's nationality, first language and date of birth. Each Overall Band Score corresponds to a descriptive statement which gives a summary of the English language ability of a candidate classified at that level. The nine bands and their descriptive statements are as follows:

9   **Expert User**—*Has fully operational command of the language: appropriate, accurate and fluent with complete understanding.*

8   **Very Good User**—*Has fully operational command of the language with only occasinal unsystematic inaccuracies and inappropriacies. Misunderstandings may occur in unfamiliar situations. Handles complex detailed argumentation well.*

7   **Good User**—*Has operational command of the language, though occasional inaccuracies, inappropriacies and misunderstandings in some situations. Generally handles complex language well and understands detailed reasoning.*

6   **Competent User**—*Has generally effective command of the language despite some inaccuracies, inappropriacies and misunderstandings. Can use and understand fairly complex language, particularly in familiar situations.*

5   **Modest User**—*Has partial command of the language, coping with overall meaning in most situations, though is likely to make many mistakes. Should be able to handle basic communication in own field.*

4   **Limited User**—*Basic competence is limited to familiar situations. Has frequent problems in understanding and expression. Is not able to use complex language.*

3   **Extremely Limited User**—*Conveys and understands only general meaning in very familiar situations. Frequent breakdowns in communication occur.*

2   **Intermittent User**—*No real communicatin is possible except for the most basic information using isolated words or short formulae in familiar situations and to meet immediate needs. Has great difficulty understanding spoken and written English.*

1   **Non User**—*Essentially has no ability to use the language beyond possibly a few isolated words.*

0   **Did not attempt the test.**—*No assessable information.*

Most universities and colleges in the United Kingdom, Australia, New Zealand and Canada accept an IELTS Overall Band Score of 6.0 or 6.5 for entry to academic programmes. IELTS scores are increasingly being recognised by Universities in the USA.

MARKING THE PRACTICE TESTS

Listening and Reading

The Answer key is on page 144.

Each item in the Listening and Reading tests is worth one mark. There are no half marks. Put a tick (√) next to each correct answer and a cross (×) next to each wrong one. Each tick will equal one mark.

Single letter / number answers

- For questions where the answer is a single letter or number, you should have written **only** one answer. If you have written more than one, the answer must be marked wrong.

Longer answers

- Only the answers given in the Answer key are correct.
- Sometimes part of the correct answer is given in brackets. Words in brackets are optional—they are correct, but not necessary.
- Alternative words or phrases within an answer are indicated by a single slash (/).
- Sometimes there are alternative correct answers to a question. In these cases the possible answers are separated by a double slash (//). If you have written any one of these possible answers, your answer is correct.
- You will find additional notes about individual questions in the Answer key.

Spelling

- Most answers require correct spelling. Where alternative spellings are acceptable, this is stated in the Answer key.
- Both US and UK spelling are acceptable.

Writing

Obviously it is not possible for you to give yourself a mark for the Writing tasks. For Tests 1, 2 and 4 and GT Test A we have provided *model answers* (written by an examiner) at the back of the book. It is important to note that these show just one way of completing the task, out of many possible approaches. For Test 3 and GT Test B we have provided *sample answers* (written by candidates), showing their score and the examiner's comments. We hope that both of these will give you an insight into what is required for the Writing module.

HOW SHOULD YOU INTERPRET YOUR SCORES?

In the Answer key at the end of the each set of Listening and Reading answers you will find a chart which will help you assess if, on the basis of your practice test results, you are ready to take the IELTS exam.

In interpreting your score, there are a number of points you should bear in mind.

Your performance in the real IELTS test will be reported in two ways: there will be a Band Score from 1 to 9 for each of the modules and an Overall Band Score from 1 to 9, which is the average of your scores in the four modules.

However, institutions considering your application are advised to look at both the Overall Band and the Bands for each module. They do this in order to see if you have the language skills needed for a particular course of study. For example, if your course has a lot of reading and writing, but no lectures, listening comprehension might be less important and a score of 5 in Listening might be acceptable if the Overall Band Score was 7. However, for a course where there are lots of lectures and spoken instructions, a score of 5 in Listening might be unacceptable even though the Overall Band Score was 7.

Once you have marked your papers you should have some idea of whether your Listening and Reading skills are good enough for you to try the real IELTS test. If you did well enough in one module but not in others, you will have to decide for yourself whether you are ready to take the proper test yet.

The Practice Tests have been checked so that they are about the same level of difficulty as the real IELTS test. However, we cannot guarantee that your score in the Practice Test papers will be reflected in the real IELTS test. The Practice Tests can only give you an idea of your possible future performance and it is ultimately up to you to make decisions based on your score.

Different institutions accept different IELTS scores for different types of courses. We have based our recommendations on the average scores which the majority of institutions accept. The institution to which you are applying may, of course, require a higher or lower score than most other institutions.

Sample answers or model answers are provided for the Writing tasks. The sample answers were written by IELTS candidates; each answer has been given a band score and the candidate's performance is described. Please note that the examiner's gridelines for marking the Writing scripts are very detailed. There are many different ways a candidate may achieve a particular band score. The model answers were written by an examiner as examples of very good answers, but it is important to understand that they are just one example out of many possible approaches.

Test 1

SECTION 1   Questions 1 – 10

Questions 1 – 5

Complete the form below.
*Write **NO MORE THAN ONE WORD OR A NUMBER** for each answer.*

VIDEO LIBRARY
APPLICATION FORM

Example	*Answer*
Surname:	Jones

First names: Louise Cynthia

Address: Apartment 1, 72 (**1**) .... street

Highbridge

Post code: (**2**) ....

Telephone: 9835 6712 (home)

(**3**) .... (work)

Driver's
licence number: (**4**) ....

Date of birth: Day: 25th Month: (**5**) .... Year: 1977

Questions 6 − 8

Circle **THREE** *letters* **A − F**.

What types of films does Louise like?
(A) Action
(B) Comedies
(C) Musicals
(D) Romance
(E) Westerns
(F) Wildlife

Questions 9 and 10

Write **NO MORE THAN THREE WORDS** *for each answer*.

9.   How much does it cost to join the library?
     ....

10. When will Louise's card be ready?
     ....

SECTION 2   *Questions 11 − 20*

Questions 11 − 13

Complete the form below.
Write **NO MORE THAN THREE WORDS** *for each answer*.

Expedition Across Attora Mountains

Leader:	Charles Owen
Prepared a	**(11)** .... for the trip
Total length of trip	**(12)** ....
Climbed highest peak in	**(13)** ....

Questions 14 and 15

Circle the correct letters **A – C.**

14. What took the group by surprise?
    (A) the amount of rain
    (B) the number of possible routes
    (C) the length of the journey

15. How did Charles feel about having to change routes?
    (A) He reluctantly accepted it.
    (B) He was irritated by the diversion.
    (C) It made no difference to his enjoyment.

Questions 16 – 18

Circle **THREE** *letters* **A – F.**

What does Charles say about his friends?
(A) He met them at one stage on the trip.
(B) They kept all their meeting arrangements.
(C) One of them helped arrange the transport.
(D) One of them owned the hotel they stayed in.
(E) Some of them travelled with him.
(F) Only one group lasted the 96 days.

Questions 19 and 20

Circle **TWO** *letters* **A – E.**

What does Charles say about the donkeys?
(A) He rode them when he was tired.
(B) He named them after places.
(C) One of them died.
(D) They behaved unpredictably.
(E) They were very small.

SECTION 3   *Questions 21 - 30*

Questions 21 - 25

Complete the form below.
Write **NO MORE THAN THREE WORDS** *for each answer.*

	TIM	JANE
Day of arrival	Sunday	(21) ....
Subject	History	(22) ....
Number of books to read	(23)	(24) ....
Day of first lecture	Tuesday	(25) ....

Questions 26 - 30

Write **NO MORE THAN THREE WORDS** *for each answer.*

26. What is Jane's study strategy in lectures?

    ....

27. What is Tim's study strategy for reading?

    ....

28. What is the subject of Tim's first lecture?

    ....

29. What is the title of Tim's first essay?

    ....

30. What is the subject of Jane's first essay?

    ....

SECTION 4   *Questions 31 - 40*

Questions 31 - 35

Complete the table below.

Write **NO MORE THAN THREE WORDS** *for each answer.*

Course	Type of course: duration and level	Entry requirements
Physical Fitness Instructor	*Example* **Six-month certificate**	None
Sports Administrator	(31)	(32) .... in sports administration
Sports Psychologist	(33)	Degree in psychology
Physical Education Teacher	Four-year degree in education	(34) ....
Recreation Officer	(35)	None

Questions 36 – 40

Complete the table below.
Write the appropriate letters **A – G** *against Questions 36 – 40.*

Job	Main role
Physical Fitness Instructor	**(36)** ....
Sports Administrator	**(37)** ....
Sports Psychologist	**(38)** ....
Physical Education Teacher	**(39)** ....
Recreation Officer	**(40)** ....

MAIN ROLES
(A)   the coaching of teams
(B)   the support of elite athletes
(C)   guidance of ordinary individuals
(D)   community health
(E)   the treatment of injuries
(F)   arranging matches and venues
(G)   the rounded development of children

READING

READING PASSAGE 1

*You should spend about 20 minutes on **Questions 1 – 13** which are based on Reading Passage 1 below.*

AIRPORTS ON WATER

River deltas are difficult places for map makers. The river builds them up, the sea wears them down; their outlines are always changing. The changes in China's Pearl River delta, however, are more dramatic than these natural fluctuations. An island six kilometres long and with a total area of 1248 hectares is being created there. And the civil engineers are as interested in performance as in speed and size. This is a bit of the delta that they want to endure.

The new island of Chek Lap Kok, the site of Hong Kong's new airport, is 83% complete. The giant dumper trucks rumbling across it will have finished their job by the middle of this year and the airport itself will be built at a similarly breakneck pace.

As Chek Lap Kok rises, however, another new Asian island is sinking back into the sea. This is a 520-hectare island built in Osaka Bay, Japan, that serves as the platform for the new Kansai airport. Chek Lap Kok was built in a different way, and thus hopes to avoid the same sinking fate.

The usual way to reclaim land is to pile sand rock on to the seabed. When the seabed oozes with mud, this is rather like placing a textbook on a wet sponge: the weight squeezes the water out, causing both water and sponge to settle lower. The settlement is rarely even: different parts sink at different rates. So buildings, pipes, roads and so on tend to buckle and crack. You can engineer around these problems, or you can engineer them out. Kansai took the first approach; Chek Lap Kok is taking the second.

The differences are both political and geological. Kansai was supposed to be built just one kilometre offshore, where the seabed is quite solid. Fishermen protested, and the site was shifted a further five kilometres. That put it in deeper water (around 20 metres) and above a seabed that consisted of 20 metres of soft alluvial silt and mud deposits. Worse, below it was a not-very-firm glacial deposit hundreds of metres thick.

The Kansai builders recognised that settlement was inevitable. Sand was driven into the seabed to strengthen it before the landfill was piled on top, in an attempt to slow the process; but this has not been as effective as had been hoped. To cope with settlement, Kansai's giant terminal is supported on 900 pillars. Each of them can be individually jacked up, allowing wedges to be added underneath. That is meant to keep the building level. But it could be a tricky task.

Conditions are different at Chek Lap Kok. There was some land there to begin with, the original little island of Chek Lap Kok and a smaller outcrop called Lam Chau. Between them, these two outcrops of hard, weathered granite make up a quarter of the new island's surface area. Unfortunately, between the islands there was a layer of soft mud, 27 metres thick in places.

According to Frans Uiterwijk, a Dutchman who is the project's reclamation director, it would have been possible to leave this mud below the reclaimed land, and to deal with the resulting settlement by the Kansai method. But the consortium that won the contract for the island opted for a more aggressive approach. It assembled the world's largest fleet of dredgers, which sucked up 150m cubic metres of clay and mud and dumped it in deeper waters. At the same time, sand was dredged from the waters and piled on top of the layer of stiff clay that the massive dredging had laid bare.

Nor was the sand the only thing used. The original granite island which had hills up to 120 metres high was drilled and blasted into boulders no bigger than two metres in diameter. This provided 70m cubic metres of granite to add to the island's foundations. Because the heap of boulders does not fill the space perfectly, this represents the equivalent of 105m cubic metres of landfill. Most of the rock will become the foundations for the airport's

runways and its taxiways. The sand dredged from the waters will also be used to provide a two-metre capping layer over the granite platform. This makes it easier for utilities to dig trenches – granite is unyielding stuff. Most of the terminal buildings will be placed above the site of the existing island. Only a limited amount of pile-driving is needed to support building foundations above softer areas.

The completed island will be six to seven metres above sea level. In all, 350m cubic metres of material will have been moved. And much of it, like the overloads, has to be moved several times before reaching its final resting place. For example, there has to be a motorway capable of carrying 150-tonne dump-trucks; and there has to be a raised area for the 15,000

construction workers. These are temporary; they will be removed when the airport is finished.

The airport, though, is here to stay. To protect it, the new coastline is being bolstered with a formidable twelve kilometres of sea defences. The brunt of a typhoon will be deflected by the neighbouring island of Lantau; the sea walls should guard against the rest. Gentler but more persistent bad weather—the downpours of the summer monsoon—is also being taken into account. A mat-like material called geotextile is being laid across the island to separate the rock and sand layers. That will stop sand particles from being washed into the rock voids, and so causing further settlement. This island is being built never to be sunk.

Questions 1 – 5

Classify the following statements as applying to

    (A) Chek Lap Kok airport only
    (B) Kansai airport only
    (C) Both airports

Write the appropriate letters **A – C** *in boxes 1 – 5 on your answer sheet.*

Example	*Answer*
built on a man-made island	**C**

1. having an area of over 1000 hectares   ~~B~~ C

2. built in a river delta   A

3. built in the open sea   B

4. built by reclaiming land   C

5. built using conventional methods of reclamation   A

Questions 6 – 9

Complete the labels on Diagam B below.
Choose your answers from the box below the diagram and write them in boxes 6 – 9 on your answer sheet.

NB *There are more words / phrases than spaces, so you will not use them all.*

DIAGRAM A
Cross-section of the original area around Chek Lap Kok before work began

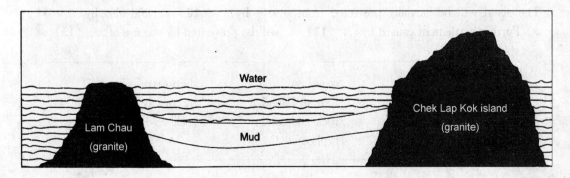

DIAGRAM B

Cross-section of the same area at the time the article was written

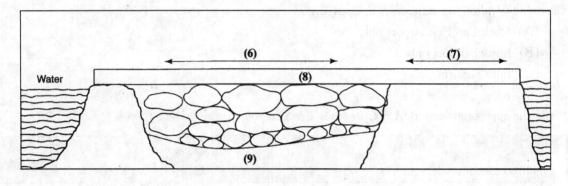

granite	runways and taxiways
mud	water
terminal building site	stiff clay
sand	

Questions 10 − 13

Complete the summary below.

Choose your answers from the box below the summary and write them in boxes 10 − 13 on your answer sheet.

NB *There are more words than spaces, so you will not use them all.*

	Answer
When the new Chek Lap Kok airport has been completed, the raised area and the... (*Example*) ...will be removed.	**motorway**

The island will be partially protected from storms by... (**10**) ...and also by... (**11**) ...Further settlement caused by... (**12**) ...will be prevented by the use of... (**13**) ...

construction workers	coastline	dump-trucks
geotextile	Lantau Island	motorway
rainfall	rock and sand	rock voids
sea walls	typhoons	

READING PASSAGE 2

You should spend about 20 minutes on **Questions 14 – 27** which are based on Reading Passage 2 on the following pages.

Questions 14 – 18

Reading Passage 2 has six paragraphs **A – F**.

Choose the most suitable headings for paragraphs **B – F** from the list of headings below.

Write the appropriate numbers (*i – iX*) in boxes 14 – 18 on your answer sheet.

NB There are more headings than paragraphs, so you will not use them all.

List of Headings
i   Ottawa International Conference on Health Promotion
ii   Holistic approach to health
iii   The primary importance of environmental factors
iV   Healthy lifestyles approach to health
V   Changes in concepts of health in Western society
Vi   Prevention of diseases and illness
Vii   Ottawa Charter for Health Promotion
Viii   Definition of health in medical terms
iX   Socio-ecological view of health

Example	Answer
Paragraph A	V

14. Paragraph **B**

15. Paragraph **C**

16. Paragraph **D**

17. Paragraph **E**

18. Paragraph **F**

Changing our Understanding of Health

A

The concept of health holds different meanings for different people and groups. These meanings of health have also changed over time. This change is no more evident than in Western society today, when notions of health and health promotion are being challenged and expanded in new ways.

B

For much of recent Western history, health has been viewed in the physical sense only. That is, good health has been connected to the smooth mechanical operation of the body, while ill health has been attributed to a breakdown in this machine. Health in this sense has been defined as the absence of disease or illness and is seen in medical terms. According to this view, creating health for people means providing medical care to treat or prevent disease and illness. During this period, there was an emphasis on providing clean water, improved sanitation and housing.

C

In the late 1940s the World Health Organistation challenged this physically and medically oriented view of health. They stated that 'health is a complete state of physical, mental and social well-being and is not merely the absence of disease' (WHO, 1946). Health and the person were seen more holistically (mind/body/spirit) and not just in physical terms.

D

The 1970s was a time of focusing on the prevention of disease and illness by emphasising the importance of the lifestyle and behaviour of the individual. Specific behaviours which were seen to increase risk of disease, such as smoking, lack of fitness and unhealthy eating habits, were targeted. Creating health meant providing not only medical health care, but health promotion programs and policies which would help people maintain healthy behaviours and lifestyles. While this individualistic healthy lifestyles approach to health worked for some (the wealthy members of society), people experiencing poverty, unemployment, underemployment or little control over the conditions of their daily lives benefited little from this approach. This was largely because both the healthy lifestyles approach and the medical approach to health largely ignored the social and environmental conditions affecting the health of people.

E

During the 1980s and 1990s there has been a growing swing away from seeing lifestyle risks as the root cause of poor health. While lifestyle factors still remain important, health is being viewed also in terms of the social, economic and environmental contexts in which people live. This broad approach to health is called the socio-ecological view of health. The broad socio-ecological view of health was endorsed at the first International Conference of Health Promotion held in 1986, Ottawa, Canada, where people from 38 countries agreed and declared that:

> The fundamental conditions and resources for health are peace, shelter, education, food, a viable income, a stable eco-system, sustainable resources, social justice and equity. Improvement in health requires a secure foundation in these basic requirements. (WHO, 1986)

It is clear from this statement that the creation of health is about much more than encouraging healthy individual behaviours and lifestyles and providing appropriate medical care. Therefore, the creation of health must include addressing issues such as poverty, pollution, urbanisation, natural resource depletion, social alienation and poor working conditions. The social, economic and environmental contexts which contribute to the creation of health do not operate separately or independently of each other. Rather, they are interacting and interdependent, and it is the complex interrelationships between them which determine the conditions that promote health. A broad socio-ecological view of health suggests that the promotion of health must include a strong social, economic and environmental focus.

F

At the Ottawa Conference in 1986, a charter was developed which outlined new directions for health promotion based on the socio-ecological view of health. This charter, known as the Ottawa Charter for Health Promotion, remains as the backbone of health action today. In exploring the scope of health promotion it states that:

> Good health is a major resource for social, economic and personal development and an important dimension of quality of life. Political, economic, social, cultural, environmental, behavioural and biological factors can all favour health or be harmful to it. (WHO, 1986)

The Ottawa Charter brings practical meaning and action to this broad notion of health promotion. It presents fundamental strategies and approaches in achieving health for all. The overall philosophy of health promotion which guides these fundamental strategies and approaches is one of 'enabling people to increase control over and to improve their health' (WHO, 1986).

Questions 19 - 22

Using **NO MORE THAN THREE WORDS** *from the passage, answer the following questions. Write your answers in boxes 19 - 22 on your answer sheet.*

19. In which year did the World Health Organisation define health in terms of mental, physical and social well-being?

20. Which members of society benefited most from the healthy lifestyles approach to health?

21. Name the three broad areas which relate to people's health, according to the socioecological view of health.

22. During which decade were lifestyle risks seen as the major contributors to poor health?

Questions 23 - 27

Do the following statements agree with the information in Reading Passage 2? In boxes 23 - 27 on your answer sheet write

> **YES**   *if the statement agrees with the information*
> **NO**   *if the statement contradicts the information*
> **NOT GIVEN**   *if there is no information on this in the passage*

23. Doctors have been instrumental in improving living standards in Western society.

24. The approach to health during the 1970s included the introduction of health awareness programs.

25. The socio-ecological view of health recognises that lifestyle habits and the provision of adequate health care are critical factors governing health.

26. The principles of the Ottawa Charter are considered to be out of date in the 1990s.

27. In recent years a number of additional countries have subscribed to the Ottawa Charter.

CHILDREN'S THINKING

One of the most eminent of psychologists, Clark Hull, claimed that the essence of reasoning lies in the putting together of two 'behaviour segments' in some novel way, never actually performed before, so as to reach a goal.

Two followers of Clark Hull, Howard and Tracey Kendler, devised a test for children that was explicitly based on Clark Hull's principles. The children were given the task of learning to operate a machine so as to get a toy. In order to succeed they had to go through a two-stage sequence. The children were trained on each stage separately. The stages consisted merely of pressing the correct one of two buttons to get a marble; and of inserting the marble into a small hole to release the toy.

The Kendlers found that the children could learn the separate bits readily enough. Given the task of getting a marble by pressing the button they could get the marble; given the task of getting a toy when a marble was handed to them, they could use the marble. (All they had to do was put it in a hole.) But they did not for the most part 'integrate', to use the Kendlers' terminology. They did not press the button to get the marble and then proceed without further help to use the marble to get the toy. So the Kendlers concluded that they were incapable of deductive reasoning.

The mystery at first appears to deepen when we learn, from another psychologist, Michael Cole, and his colleagues, that adults in an African culture apparently cannot do the Kendlers' task either. But it lessens, on the other hand, when we learn that a task was devised which was strictly analogous to the Kendlers' one but much easier for the African males to handle.

Instead of the button-pressing machine, Cole used a locked box and two differently coloured match-boxes, one of which contained a key that would open the box. Notice that there are still two behaviour segments— 'open the right match-box to get the key' and 'use the key to open the box' —so the task seems formally to be the same. But psychologically it is quite different. Now the subject is dealing not with a strange machine but with familiar meaningful objects; and it is clear to him what he is meant to do. It then turns out that the difficulty of 'integration' is greatly reduced.

Recent work by Simon Hewson is of great interest here for it shows that, for young children, too, the difficulty lies not in the inferential processes which the task demands, but in certain perplexing features of the apparatus and the procedure. When these are changed in ways which do not at all affect the inferential nature of the problem, then five-year-old children solve the problem as well as college students did in the Kendlers' own experiments.

Hewson made two crucial changes. First, he replaced the button-pressing mechanism in the side panels by drawers in these panels which the child could open and shut. This took away the mystery from the first stage of training. Then he helped the child to understand that there was no 'magic' about the specific marble which, during the second stage of training, the experimenter handed to him so that the he could pop it in the hole and get the reward.

A child understands nothing, after all, about how a marble put into a hole can open a little door. How is he to know that any other marble of similar size will do just as well? Yet he must assume that if he is to solve the problem. Hewson made the functional equivalence of different marbles clear by playing a 'swapping game' with the children.

The two modifications together produced a jump in success rates from 30 per cent to 90 per cent for five-year-olds and from 35 per cent to 72.5 per cent for four-year-olds. For three-year-olds, for reasons that are still in need of clarification, no improvement – rather a slight drop in performance – resulted from the change.

We may conclude, then that children experience very real difficulty when faced with the Kendler apparatus; but this difficulty cannot be taken as proof that they are incapable of deductive reasoning.

Questions 28 – 35

Classify the following descriptions as referring to

Clark Hull	**CH**
Howard and Tracey Kendler	**HTK**
Michael Cole and colleagues	**MC**
Simon Hewson	**SH**

Write the appropriate letters in boxes 28 – 35 on your answer sheet.

NB *You may use any answer more than once.*

28. .... is cited as famous in the field of psychology.

29. .... demonstrated that the two-stage experiment involving button-pressing and inserting a marble into a hole poses problems for certain adults as well as children.

30. .... devised an experiment that investigated deductive reasoning without the use of any marbles.

31. .... appears to have proved that a change in the apparatus dramatically improves the performance of children of certain ages.

32. .... used a machine to measure inductive reasoning that replaced button-pressing with drawer-opening.

33. .... experimented with things that the subjects might have been expected to encounter in everyday life, rather than with a machine.

34. .... compared the performance of five-year-olds with college students, using the same apparatus with both sets of subjects.

35. .... is cited as having demonstrated that earlier experiments into children's ability to reason deductively may have led to the wrong conclusions.

Questions 36 – 40

*Do the following statements agree with the information given in Reading Passage 3? In boxes 36 –
40 on you answer sheet write.*

YES	*if the statement agrees with the information*
NO	*if the statement contradicts the information*
NOT GIVEN	*if there is no information on this in the passage*

36. Howard and Tracey Kendler studied under Clark Hull.

37. The Kendlers trained their subjects separately in the two stages of their experiment, but not in how to integrate the two actions.

38. Michael Cole and his colleagues demonstrated that adult performance on inductive reasoning tasks depends on features of the apparatus and procedure.

39. All Hewson's experiments used marbles of the same size.

40. Hewson's modifications resulted in a higher success rate for children of all ages.

WRITING

WRITING TASK 1

You should spend about 20 minutes on this task.

> **The table below shows the consumer durables (telephone, refrigerator, etc.) owned in Britain from 1972 to 1983.**
>
> **Write a report for a university lecturer describing the information shown below.**

You should write at least 150 words.

Consumer durables	1972	1974	1976	1978	1979	1981	1982	1983
Percentage of households with:								
central heating	37	43	48	52	55	59	60	64
television	93	95	96	96	97	97	97	98
video								18
vacuum cleaner	87	89	92	92	93	94	95	
refrigerator	73	81	88	91	92	93	93	94
washing machine	66	68	71	75	74	78	79	80
dishwasher				3	3	4	4	5
telephone	42	50	54	60	67	75	76	77

WRITING TASK 2

You should spend about 40 minutes on this task.

Present a written argument or case to an educated reader with no specialist knowledge of the following topic.

> *"Fatherhood ought to be emphasised as much as motherhood. The idea that women are solely responsible for deciding whether or not to have babies leads on to the idea that they are also responsible for bringing the children up."*
>
> *To what extent do you agree or disagree?*

You should write at least 250 words.

You should use your own ideas, knowledge and experience and support your arguments with examples and relevant evidence.

Task:

The candidate is to find out as much information as possible about electronic mail.

Candidate's cue card:

ELECTRONIC MAIL

You are studying at a language school and have heard that students may obtain an electronic mail (e-mail) address so that they can send and receive messages by computer. The Examiner is the Student Services advisor.

Ask the Examiner about: what e-mail is

cost

how to obtain an e-mail address

location of e-mail at school

equipment needed at home

courses on e-mail

Information for the Examiner:

what e-mail is .... means by which to send messages from one computer to another over the telephone lines

cost .... free for students at this language school

how to obtain an e-mail address .... complete an application form and return to Student Services

location of a e-mail at school .... in the independent learning centre or computer laboratory

equipment needed at home .... a modem and a telephone line

courses on e-mail .... Friday afternoon classes throughout the year

Test 2

SECTION 1 Questions 1 – 10

Questions 1 and 2

Circle the correct letters **A – C**.

> *Example*
> Gavin moved into his apartment...
>   (A)   two days ago.
>   ☐(B)   two weeks ago.
>   (C)   two months ago.

1. Gavin's apartment is located on the _____.
   (A) ground floor.
   (B) second floor.
   (C) third floor.

2. The monthly rent for Gavin's apartment is _____.
   (A) $ 615.
   (B) $ 650.
   (C) $ 655.

Questions 3 – 6

Complete the table below.
Write **NO MORE THAN THREE WORDS** *for each answer.*

ITEM	VALUE
(3)	$ 450
(4)	$ 1,150
Watches	$ 2,000
CDs and **(5)**	$ 400
Total annual **cost** of insurance **(6)** $	

Complete the form below.
Write **NO MORE THAN THREE WORDS** *for each answer.*

INSURANCE
APPLICATION FORM

Name: *Mr Gavin* **(7)** ....

Address: **(8)** .... *Biggins Street*

                   (9) ....

Date of Birth: *12th November* 1980

Telephone: Home: 9872 4855

Nationality: **(10)** ....

SECTION 2   *Questions 11 – 20*

Questions 11

Circle the correct letter **A – D**.

Smith House was originally built as _____
(A) a residential college.
(B) a family house.
(C) a university.
(D) an office block.

Questions 12 – 14

Complete the explanation of the room number.
Write **NO MORE THAN THREE WORDS** *for each answer.*

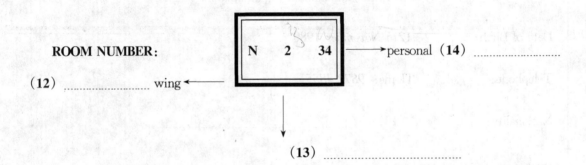

ROOM NUMBER: N   2   34 ──→personal **(14)** ....

(12) .... wing ←

(13) ....

Questions 15 – 17

Complete the sentences below.
Write **NO MORE THAN THREE WORDS** *for each answer.*

• Students need a front door key between **(15)** .... AND ....
• In an emergency, students should use **(16)** ....
• Fees also cover some **(17)** .... charges.

Questions 18 − 20

Complete the sentences below.
Write NO MORE THAN THREE WORDS for each answer.

HOUSE RULES

°₀°₀

- **No noise after 9 pm.**
- **Smoking only allowed on (18)** ....
- **No changes can be made to (19)** ....
- *If you have any questions, ask the (20)* ....

SECTION 3   *Questions 21 − 30*

Questions 21 − 25

Complete the form below.
Write NO MORE THAN THREE WORDS for each answer.

Forms of media	Examples
Print	• books
	• (21) ....
Pictures	• (22) ....
Audio (listening)	• CDs
	• (23) ....
Audio-visual	• film
	• (24) ....
	• videos
Electronic	(25) ....

Questions 26 - 30

Write the appropriate letters **A** - **C** *against questions 26 - 30*.

According to the speakers, in which situation are the following media most useful?

    (A) individual children
    (B) five or six children
    (C) whole class

Example	Answer
pictures	A

26. tapes   ....
27. computers   ....
28. videos   ....
29. books   ....
30. wall maps   ....

SECTION 4   *Questions 31 - 40*

Questions 31

Circle the correct letter **A** - **D**.

What percentage of the workforce were employed in agriculture in the mid 1900s?

(A) 30%
(B) 10%
(C) 20%
(D) 50%

Questions 32 and 33

Complete the notes below:

Write **NO MORE THAN THREE WORDS** *for each answer*.

Three factors contributing to the efficiency of the agricultural sector are...

* 50 - 60 years of intelligent state support
* the quality of (**32**) .... among those employed
* the farmers' investment in (**33**) ....

Questions 34 – 39

Complete the table below :

Write **NO MORE THAN THREE WORDS** *for each answer .*

Region	North	East	West
Land	hilly with thin soil	flat with (**36**)	rich soil
Climate	(**34**) .... and	mixed	(**38**) .... and ....
Farm type	small, family-run	commercial	average size (**39**) .... hectares
Produce	(**35**) .... and	cereals and (**37**)	milk, cheese and meat

Questions 40

Circle the correct letter **A – C.**

Farmers have a strong sense of solidarity because _____

(A) the media supports them.

(B) they have a strong Union.

(C) they have countrywide interests.

READING PASSAGE 1

You should spend about 20 minutes on **Questions 1 – 13** *which are based on Reading Passage 1 below.*

IMPLEMENTING THE CYCLE OF SUCCESS: A CASE STUDY

Within Australia, Australian Hotels Inc (AHI) operates nine hotels and employs over 2000 permanent full-time staff, 300 permanent part-time employees and 100 casual staff. One of its latest ventures, the Sydney Airport hotel (SAH), opened in March 1995. The hotel is the closest to Sydney Airport and is designed to provide the best available accommodation, food and beverage and meeting facilities in Sydney's southern suburbs. Similar to many international hotel chains, however, AHI has experienced difficulties in Australia in providing long-term profits for hotel owners, as a result of the country's high labour-cost structure. In order to develop an economically viable hotel organisation model, AHI decided to implement some new policies and practices at SAH.

The first of the initiatives was an organisational structure with only three levels of management—compared to the traditional seven. Partly as a result of this change, there are 25 per cent fewer management positions, enabling a significant saving. This change also has other implications. Communication, both up and down the organisation, has greatly improved. Decision-making has been forced down in many cases to front-line employees. As a result, guest requests are usu-

ally met without reference to a supervisor, improving both customer and employee satisfaction.

The hotel also recognised that it would need a different approach to selecting employees who would fit in with its new policies. In its advertisements, the hotel stated a preference for people with some 'service' experience in order to minimise traditional work practices being introduced into the hotel. Over 7000 applicants filled in application forms for the 120 jobs initially offered at SAH. The balance of the positions at the hotel (30 management and 40 shift leader positions) were predominantly filled by transfers from other AHI properties.

A series of tests and interviews were conducted with potential employees, which eventually left 280 applicants competing for the 120 advertised positions. After the final interview, potential recruits were divided into three categories. Category A was for applicants exhibiting strong leadership qualities, Category C was for applicants perceived to be followers, and Category B was for applicants with both leader and follower qualities. Department heads and shift leaders then composed prospective teams using a combination of people from all three categories. Once suitable teams were formed, offers of employment were made to team members.

Another major initiative by SAH was to adopt a totally multi-skilled workforce. Although there may be some limitations with highly technical jobs such as cooking or maintenance, wherever possible, employees at SAH are able to work in a wide variety of positions. A multi-skilled workforce provides far greater management flexibilyty during peak and quiet times to transfer employees to needed positions. For example, when office staff are away on holidays during quiet periods of the year, employees in either food or beverage or housekeeping departments can temporarily fill in.

The most crucial way, however, of improving the labour cost structure at SAH was to find better, more productive ways of providing customer service. SAH management concluded this would first require a process of 'benchmarking'. The prime objective of the benchmarking process was to compare a range of service delivery processes across a range of criteria using teams made up of employees from different departments within the hotel which interacted with each other. This process resulted in performance measures that greatly enhanced SAH's ability to improve productivity and quality.

The front office team discovered through this project that a high proportion of AHI Club member reservations were incomplete. As a result, the service provided to these guests was below the sandard promised to them as part of their membership agreement. Reducing the number of incomplete reservations greatly improved guest perceptions of service.

In addition, a program modelled on an earlier project called 'Take Charge' was implemented. Essentially, Take Charge provides an effective feedback loop from both customers and employees. Customer comments, both positive and negative, are recorded by staff. These are collated regularly to identify opportunities for improvement. Just as importantly, employees are requested to note down their own suggestions for improvement. (AHI has set an expectation that employees will submit at least three suggestions for every one they receive from a customer.) Employee feedback is reviewed daily and suggestions are implemented within 48 hours, if possible, or a valid reason is given for non-implementation. If suggestions require analysis or data collection, the Take Charge team has 30 days in which to address the issue and come up with recommendations.

Although quantitative evidence of AHI's initiatives at SAH are limited at present, anecdotal evidence clearly suggests that these practices are working. Indeed AHI is progressively rolling out these initiatives in other hotels in Australia, whilst numerous overseas visitors have come to see how the program works.

This article has been adapted and condensed from the article by R.Carter (1996), 'Implementing the cycle of success: A case study of the Sheraton Pacific Division', *Asia Pacific Journal of Human Resources*, 34(3):111-23. Names and other details have been changed and report findings may have been given a different emphasis from the original. We are grateful to the author and *Asia Pacific Journal of Human Resources* for allowing us to use the material in this way.

Questions 1 – 5

*Choose the appropriate letters **A – D** and write them in boxes 1 – 5 on your answer sheet.*

1. The high costs of running AHI's hotels are related to their _____
   (A) management.
   (B) size.
   (C) staff.
   (D) policies.

2. SAH's new organisational structure requires _____
   (A) 75% of the old management positions.
   (B) 25% of the old management positions.
   (C) 25% more management positions.
   (D) 5% fewer management positions.

3. The SAH's approach to organisational structure required changing practices in _____
   (A) industrial relations.
   (B) firing staff.
   (C) hiring staff.
   (D) marketing.

4. The total number of jobs advertised at the SAH was _____
   (A) 70.
   (B) 120.
   (C) 170.
   (D) 280.

5. Categories A, B and C were used to select _____
   (A) front office staff.
   (B) new teams.
   (C) department heads.
   (D) new managers.

Questions 6 - 13

Complete the following summary of the last **four** paragraphs of Reading Passage 1 using **ONE OR TWO** words from the Rdading Passage for each answer.
Write you answers in boxes 6 - 13 on your answer sheet.

WHAT THEY DID AT SAH

Teams of employees were selected from different hotel departments to participate in a... (**6**) ...exercise.

The information collected was used to compare... (**7**) ...processes which, in turn, led to the development of... (**8**) ...that would be used to increase the hotel's capacity to improve... (**9**) ...as well as quality.

Also, and older program known as... (**10**) ...was introduced at SAH. In this program, ... (**11**) ...is sought from customers and staff. Wherever possible... (**12**) ...suggestions are implemented within 48 hours. Other suggestions are investigated for their feasibility for a period of up to... (**13**) ....

READING PASSAGE 2

*You should spend about 20 minutes on **Questions 14 – 26** which are based on Reading Passage 2 below.*

The discovery that language can be a barrier to communication is quickly made by all who travel, study, govern or sell. Whether the activity is tourism, research, government, policing, business, or data dissemination, the lack of a common language can severely impede progress or can halt it altogether. 'Common language' here usually means a foreign language, but the same point applies in principle to any encounter with unfamiliar dialects or styles within a single language. 'They don't talk the same language' has a major metaphorical meaning alongside its literal one.

Although communication problems of this kind must happen thousands of times each day, very few become public knowledge. Publicity comes only when a failure to communicate has major consequences, such as strikes, lost orders, legal problems, or fatal accidents – even, at times, war. One reported instance of communication failure took place in 1970, when several Americans ate a species of poisonous mushroom. No remedy was known, and two of the people died within days. A radio report of the case was heard by a chemist who knew of a treatment that had been successfully used in 1959 and published in 1963. Why had the American doctors not heard of it seven years later? Presumably because the report of the treatment had been published only in journals written in European languages other than English.

Several comparable cases have been reported. But isolated examples do not give an impression of the size of the problem – something that can come only from studies of the use or avoidance of foreign-language materials and contacts in different communicative situations. In the English-speaking scientific world, for example, surveys of books and documents consulted in libraries and other information agencies have shown that very little foreign-language material is ever consulted. Library requests in the field of science and technology showed that only 13 per cent were for foreign language periodicals. Studies of the sources cited in publications lead to a similar conclusion: the use of foreign-language sources is often found to be as low as 10 per cent.

The language barrier presents itself in stark form to firms who wish to market their products in other countries. British industry, in particular, has in recent decades often been criticised for its linguistic insularity – for its assumption that foreign buyers will be happy to communicate in English, and that awareness of other languages is not therefor a priorty. In the 1960s, over two-thirds of British firms dealing with non-English-speaking customers were using English for outgoing correspondence; many had their sales literature only in English; and as many as 40 per cent employed no-one able to communicate in the customers' languages, A similar problem was identified in other English-speaking countries, notably the USA, Australia and New Zealand. And non-English-speaking countries were by no means exempt – although the widespread use of English as an alternative language made them less open to the charge of insularity.

The criticism and publicity given to this problem since the 1960s seems to have greatly improved the situation. Industrial training schemes have promoted an increase in linguistic and cultural awareness. Many firms now have their own translation services; to take just one example in Britain, Rowntree Mackintosh now publish their documents in six languages (English, French, German, Dutch, Italian and Xhosa). Some firms run part-time language courses in the languages of the countries with which they are most involved; some produce their own technical glossaries, to ensure consistency when material is being translated. It is now much more readily appreciated that marketing efforts can be delayed, damaged, or disrupted by a failure to take account of the linguistic needs of the customer.

The changes in awareness have been most marked in English-speaking countries, where the realisation has gradually dawned that by no means everyone in the world knows English well enough to negotiate in it. This is especially a problem when English is not an official language of public administration, as in most parts of the Far East, Russia, Eastern Europe, the Arab would, Latin America and French-speaking Africa. Even in cases where foreign customers can speak English quite well, it is often forgotten that they may not be able to understand it to the required level – bearing in mind the regional and social variation which permeates speech and which can cause major problems of listening comprehension. In securing understanding, how ‘we’ speak to ‘them’ is just as important, it appears, as how ‘they’ speak to ‘us’.

Questions 14 - 17

Complete each of the following statements (Questions 14 - 17) with words taken from Reading Passage 2.
*Write **NO MORE THAN THREE WORDS** for each answer.*
Write your answers in boxes 14 - 17 on your answer sheet.

14. Language problems may come to the attention of the public when they have ...., such as fatal accidents or social problems.

15. Evidence of the extent of the language barrier has been gained from .... of materials used by scientists such as books and periodicals.

16. An example of British linguistic insularity is the use of English for materials such as ....

17. An example of a part of the world where people may have difficulty in negotiating English is ....

Questions 18 - 20

Choose the appropriate letter A - D and write them in boxes 18 - 20 on your answer sheet.

18. According to the passage, 'They don't talk the same language' (paragraph 1), can refer to problems in _____
    (A) understanding metaphor.
    (B) learning foreign languages.
    (C) understanding dialect or style.
    (D) dealing with technological change.

19. The case of the poisonous mushrooms (paragraph 2) suggests that American doctors _____
    (A) should pay more attention to radio reports.
    (B) only read medical articles if they are in English.
    (C) are sometimes unwilling to try foreign treatments.
    (D) do not always communicate effectively with their patients.

20. According to the writer, the linguistic insularity of British businesses _____
    (A) later spread to other countries.
    (B) had a negative effect on their business.
    (C) is not as bad now as it used to be in the past
    (D) made non-English-speaking companies turn to other markets.

Questions 21 - 24

List the **FOUR** main ways in which British companies have tried to solve the problem of the language barrier since the 1960s.
Write **NO MORE THAN THREE WORDS** for each answer.
Write your answers in boxes 21 - 24 on your answer sheet.

21. ....

22. ....

23. ....

24. ....

Questions 25 and 26

Choose the appropriate letters **A - D** and write them in boxes 25 and 26 on your answer sheet.

25. According to the writer, English-speaking people need to be aware that _____
    (A) some foreigners have never met an English-speaking person.
    (B) many foreigners have no desire to learn English.
    (C) foreign language may pose a greater problem in the future.
    (D) English-speaking foreigners may have difficulty understanding English.

26. A suitable title for this passage would be _____
    (A) Overcoming the language barrier
    (B) How to survive an English-speaking world
    (C) Global understanding – the key to personal progress
    (D) The need for a common language

READING PASSAGE 3

You should spend about 20 minutes on **Questions 27 - 40** *which are based on Reading Passage 3 on the following pages.*

Questions 27 - 30

Reading Passage 3 has seven paragraphs **A - G.**
From the list of headings below choose the most suitable headings for paragraphs **B - E.**
Write the appropriate numbers (*i - viii*) *in boxes 27 - 30 on your answer sheet.*

NB *There are more headings than paragraphs, so you will not use them all.*

List of Headings

i   A truly international environment
ii   Once a port city, always a port city
iii Good ports make huge profits
iv How the port changes a city's infrastructure
v   Reasons for the decline of ports
vi Relative significance of trade and service industry
vii Ports and harbours
viii The demands of the oil industry

Example	Answer
Paragraph A	vii

27. Paragraph **B**

28. Paragraph **C**

29. Paragraph **D**

30. Paragraph **E**

What is a Port City?

The port city provides a fascinating and rich understanding of the movement of people and goods around the world. We understand a port as a centre of land-sea exchange, and as a major source of livelihood and a major force for cultural mixing. But do ports all produce a range of common urban characteristics which justify classifying port cities together under a single generic label? Do they have enough in common to warrant distinguishing them from other kinds of cities?

A   A port must be distinguished from a harbour. They are two very different things. Most ports have poor harbours, and many fine harbours see few ships. Harbour is a physical concept, a shelter for ships; port is an economic concept, a centre of land-sea exchange which requires good access to a hinterland even more than a sea-linked foreland. it is landward access, which is productive of goods for export and which demands imports, that is critical. Poor harbours can be improved with breakwaters and dredging if there is a demand for a port. Madras and Colombo are examples of harbours expensively improved by enlarging, dredging and building breakwaters.

B   Port cities become industrial, financial and service centres and political capitals because of their water connections and the urban concentration which arises there and later draws to it railways, highways and air routes. Water transport means cheap access, the chief basis of all port cities. Many of the world's biggest cities, for example, London, New York, Shanghai, Istanbul, Buenos Aires, Tokyo, Jakarta, Calcutta, Philadelphia and San Francisco began as ports – that is, with land-sea exchange as their major function – but they have since grown disproportionately in other respects so that their port functions are no longer dominant. They remain different kinds of places from non-port cities and their port functions account for that difference.

C   Port functions, more than anything else, make a city cosmopolitan. A port city is open to the world. In it races, cultures, and ideas, as well as goods from a variety of places, jostle, mix and enrich each other and the life of the city. The smell of the sea and the harbour, the sound of boat whistles or the moving tides are symbols of their multiple links with a wide world, samples of which are present in microcosm within their own urban areas.

D   Sea ports have been transformed by the advent of powered vessels, whose size and draught have increased. Many formerly important ports have become economically and physically less accessible as a result. By-passed by most of their former enriching flow of exchange, they have become cultural and economic backwaters or have acquired the character of museums of the past. Examples of these are Charleston, Salem, Bristol, Plymouth, Surat, Galle, Melaka, Suzhou chow, and a long list of earlier prominent port cities in Southeast Asia, Africa and Latin America.

E Much domestic port trade has not been recorded. What evidence we have suggests that domestic trade was greater at all periods than external trade. Shanghai, for example, did most of its trade with other Chinese ports and inland cities. Calcutta traded mainly with other parts of India and so on. Most of any city's population is engaged in providing goods and services for the city itself. Trade outside the city is its basic function. But each basic worker requires food, housing, clothing and other such services. Estimates of the ratio of basic to service workers range from 1:4 to 1:8.

F No city can be simply a port but must be involved in a variety of other activities. The port function of the city draws to it raw materials and distributes them in many other forms. Ports take advantage of the need for breaking up the bulk material where water and land transport meet and where loading and unloading costs can be minimised by refining raw materials or turning them into finished goods. The major examples here are oil refining and ore refining, which are commonly located at ports. It is not easy to draw a line around what is and is not a port function. All ports handle, unload, sort, alter, process, repack, and reship most of what they receive. A city may still be regarded as a port city when it becomes involved in a great range of functions not immediately involved with ships or docks.

G Cities which began as ports retain the chief commercial and administrative centre of the city close to the waterfront. The centre of New York is in lower Manhattan between two river mouths, the City of London is on the Thames, Shanghai along the Bund. This proximity to water is also true of Boston, Philadelphia, Bombay, Calcutta, Madras, Singapore, Bangkok, Hong Kong and Yokohama, where the commercial, financial, and administrative centres are still grouped around their harbours even though each city has expanded into a metropolis. Even a casual visitor cannot mistake them as anything but port cities.

Questions 31 – 34

Look at the following descriptions (**Questions 31 – 34**) of some port cities mentioned in Reading Passage 3.

Match the pairs of cities (**A – H**) listed below, with the descriptions.
Write the appropriate letters **A – H** in boxes 31 – 34 on your answer sheet.

NB   There are more pairs of port cities than descriptions. so you will not use them all.

31. required considerable harbour development

32. began as ports but other facilities later dominated

33. lost their prominence when large ships could not be accommodated

34. maintain their business centres near the port waterfront

(A) Bombay and Buenos Aires
(B) Hong Kong and Salem
(C) Istanbul and Jakarta
(D) Madras and Colombo
(E) New York and Bristol
(F) Plymouth and Melaka
(G) Singapore and Yokohama
(H) Surat and London

Questions 35 – 40

Do the following statements agree with the information given in Reading Passage 3?
In boxes 35 – 40 on your answer sheet write

YES   if the statement agrees with the information
NO   if the statement contradicts the information
NOT GIVEN if there is no information on this in the passage

35. Cities cease to be port cities when other functions dominate.

36. In the past, many cities did more trade within their own country than with overseas ports.

37. Most people in a port city are engaged in international trade and finance.

38. Ports attract many subsidiary and independent industries.

39. Ports have to establish a common language of trade.

40. Ports often have river connections.

WRITING

WRITING TASK 1

You should spend about 20 minutes on this task.

> *The chart below shows the amount of leisure time enjoyed by men and women of different employment status.*
>
> *Write a report for a university lecturer describing the information shown below.*

You should write at least 150 wrods.

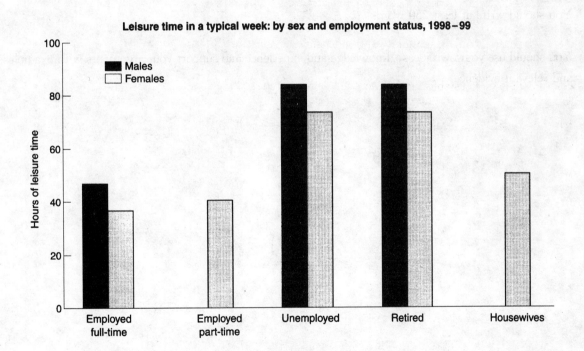

Leisure time in a typical week: by sex and employment status, 1998–99

WRITING TASK 2

You should spend about 40 minutes on this task.

Present a written argument or case to an educated reader with no specialist knowledge of the following topic.

"*Prevention is better than cure.*"

Out of a country's health budget, a large proportion should be diverted from treatment to spending on health education and preventative measures.

To what extent do you agree of disagree with this statement?

You should write at least 250 words.

You should use your own ideas, knowledge and experience and support your arguments with examples and relevant evidence.

Task:

The candidate is to find out as much information as possible about a concert.

Candidate's cue card:

CONCERT

Find out as much as possible about a concert your examiner has been to recently.

Ask the examiner about: the type of concert

the location

the cost

transport to and from the concert

the audience

the length of the concert

his/her opinion of the concert

Information for the Examiner:

the type of concert	rock/folk/jazz/classical
the location	city stadium
the cost	$55/£25
transport to and from the concert	bus (hard to park car)
the audience	500 – 1,000 people, lots of audience participation
The length of the concert	3 hours
his/her opinion of the concert	really enjoyed it

Test 3

LISTENING

SECTION 1   Questions 1 – 10

Questions 1 – 4

Circle the correct letters **A** – **C**.

> *Example*
> The respondent is...
>   (A)   20 – 23 years old.
>   [(B)]   34 – 53 years old.
>   (C)   over 54 years old.

1. The respondent works on _____
   (A) the professions.
   (B) business.
   (C) other.

2. The respondent has a salary of _____
   (A) 0 – £ 15,000 a year.
   (B) £ 15,000 – £ 35,000 a year.
   (C) over £ 35,000 a year.

3. The respondent watches TV for _____
   (A) relaxation.
   (B) entertainment.
   (C) information.

4. Every day the respondent watches TV for _____
   (A) 30 minutes – 1 hour.
   (B) 1 hour – 2 hours.
   (C) more than 2 hours.

Questions 5 – 7

*Choose **TWO** letters **A** – **E**.*

5. The respondent mainly watches **TV** _____
   - (A) in the early morning.
   - (B) around midday.
   - (C) in the afternoon.
   - (D) in the early evening.
   - (E) at night.

6. On the new channel, the respondent would like to see more _____
   - (A) children's programmes.
   - (B) documentaries.
   - (C) local service programmes.
   - (D) travel programmes.
   - (E) health programmes.

7. The respondent would advise the new channel to _____
   - (A) spend more money on drama.
   - (B) train their broadcasters to higher standards.
   - (C) improve sound quality.
   - (D) broadcast interviews with famous people.
   - (E) talk more to customers.

Questions 8 – 10

*Circle the correct letters **A** – **C**.*

8. The respondent feels that adverts should occur every _____
   - (A) 10 minutes.
   - (B) 15 minutes.
   - (C) 20 minutes.

9. The respondent would like to attend special special promotions if _____
   - (A) expenses are paid.
   - (B) he is invited specially.
   - (C) they are held locally.

10. The respondent would like to receive _____
    - (A) no mail.
    - (B) requested mail.
    - (C) all mail.

SECTION 2   *Questions 11 – 20*

Questions 11 – 14

Circle **FOUR** *letters* **A – G**.

Which **FOUR** activities of the Union are mentioned by the speaker?

(A) raising money for good causes

(B) political campaigning

(C) running a newsagent's

(D) running a supermarket

(E) providing cheap tickets

(F) helping with accommodation

(G) providing catering services

Questions 15 and 16

circle **TWO** *letters* **A – E**.

Which **TWO** of the following can you get advice about from the Union?

(A) immigration

(B) grants

(C) medical problems

(D) personal problems

(E) legal matters

Questions 17 – 20

*Write the appropriate letters **A – C** against Questions 17 – 20.*

What are the locations of the following places in Radford?

    (A) part of the Metro Tower building

    (B) in the main square in the centre of the town

    (C) some distance from the centre of the town

Example	Answer
the swimming pool	C

17. The hi-tech fitness centre   ....

18. the ice rink   ....

19. the new cinema   ....

20. the Theatre Royal   ....

SECTION 3

Questions 21 − 30

Questions 21 − 23

Complete the notes below.
*Write **NO MORE THAN THREE WORDS** or **A NUMBER** for each answer.*

DISSERTATION INFORMATION

Hand-in date: **(21)** ....

Length: **(22)** .... to .... words

Extra programme offered on: **(23)** ....

Questions 24 − 26

Complete the table below.

DISSERTATION TIMETABLE

Date	Action
31 January	Basic bibliography
7 February	**(24)** ....
February-March	**(25)** ....
(26) .... to	Write up work
21 May	Hand in work

Questions 27 – 30

What is Dr Simon's opinion on the following points?

Tick column A   *if he is in favour*
Tick column B   *if he has no strong opinion either way*
Tick column C   *if he is against*

	A	B	C
(27) Buying a computer			
(28) Reading previous year's dissertations			
(29) Using questionnaires as main research instrument			
(30) Interviewing tutors			

SECTION 4   *Questions 31 - 40*

Questions 31 - 37

Circle the correct letters **A - C.**

31. The driest continents is _____
    (A) Australia.
    (B) Africa.
    (C) Antarctica.

32. The evaporation rate in Australia is _____
    (A) lower than Africa.
    (B) higher than Africa.
    (C) about the same as Africa.

33. Rainfall in Australia hardly penetrates the soil because _____
    (A) the soil is too hard.
    (B) the soil is too hot.
    (C) plants use it up.

34. In sandy soils water can _____
    (A) evaporate quickly.
    (B) seep down to rock.
    (C) wash the soil away.

35. Water is mainly pumped up for _____
    (A) people to drink.
    (B) animals to drink.
    (C) watering crops.

36. Natural springs are located _____
    (A) in unexplored parts of Australia.
    (B) quite commonly over all Australia.
    (C) in a few areas of Australia.

37. Underground water supplies _____.
    (A) 18% of Australia's water.
    (B) 48% of Australia's water.
    (C) 80% of Australia's water.

Questions 38 – 40

Circle **THREE** *letters* **A – E**.

Which **THREE** of the following uses of dam water are mentioned?
(A) providing water for livestock
(B) watering farmland
(C) providing water for industry
(D) controlling flood water
(E) producing hydro-electric power

READING

READING PASSAGE 1

You should spend about 20 *minutes on* **Questions 1 − 13** *which are based on Reading Passage* **1** *below.*

ABSENTEEISM IN NURSING: A LONGITUDINAL STUDY

Absence from work is a costly and disruptive problem for any organisation. The cost of absenteeism in Australia has been put at 1.8 million hours per day or $ 1400 million annually. The study reported here was conducted in the Prince William Hospital in Brisbane, Australia, where, prior to this time, few active steps had been taken to measure, understand or manage the occurrence of absenteeism.

Nursing Absenteeism
A prevalent attitude amongst many nurses in the group selected for study was that there was no reward or recognition for not utilising the paid sick leave entitlement allowed them in their employment conditions. Therefore, they believed they may as well take the days off − sick or otherwise. Similar attitudes have been noted by James (1989), who noted that sick leave is seen by many workers as a right, like annual holiday leave.

Miller and Norton (1986), in their survey of 865 nursing personnel, found that 73 per cent felt they should be rewarded for not taking sick leave, because some employees always used their sick leave. Further, 67 per cent of nurses felt that administration was not sympathetic to the problems shift work causes to employees' personal and social lives. Only 53 per cent of

the respondents felt that every effort was made to schedule staff fairly.

In another longitudinal study of nurses working in two Canadian hospitals, Hackett, Bycio and Guion (1989) examined the reasons why nurses took absence from work. The most frequent reason stated for absence was minor illness to self. Other causes, in decreasing order of frequency, were illness in family, family social function, work to do at home and bereavement.

Method
In an attempt to reduce the level of absenteeism amongst the 250 Registered and Enrolled Nurses in the present study, the Prince William management introduced three different, yet potentially complementary, strategies over 18 months.

Strategy 1: *Non-financial (material) incentives*
Within the established wage and salary system it was not possible to use hospital funds to support this strategy. However, it was possible to secure incentives from local businesses, including free passes to entertainment parks, theatres, restaurants, etc. At the end of each roster period, the ward with the lowest

absence rate would win the prize.

Strategy 2: Flexible fair rostering Where possible, staff were given the opportunity to determine their working schedule within the limits of clinical needs.

Strategy 3: Individual absenteeism and counselling

Each month, managers would analyse the pattern of absence of staff with excessive sick leave (greater than ten days per year for full-time employees). Characteristic patterns of potential 'voluntary absenteeism' such as absence before and after days off, excessive weekend and night duty absence and multiple single days off were communicated to all ward nurses and then, as necessary, followed up by action.

Results

Absence rates for the six months prior to the incentive scheme ranged from 3.69 per cent to 4.32 per cent. In the following six months they ranged between 2.87 per cent and 3.96 per cent. This represents a 20 per cent improvement. However, analysing the absence rates on a year-to-year basis, the overall absence rate was 3.60 per cent in the first year and 3.43 per cent in the following year. This represents a 5 per cent decrease from the first to the second year of the study. A significant decrease in absence over the two-year period could not be demonstrated.

Discussion

The non-financial incentive scheme did appear to assist in controlling absenteeism in the short term. As the scheme progressed it became harder to secure prizes and this contributed to

the program's losing momentum and finally ceasing. There were mixed results across wards as well. For example, in wards with staff members who had long-term genuine illness, there was little chance of winning, and to some extent the staff on those wards were disempowered. Our experience would suggest that the long-term effects of incentive awards on absenteeism are questionable.

Over the time of the study, staff were given a larger detree of control in their rosters. This led to significant improvements in communication between managers and staff. A similar effect was found from the implementation of the third strategy. Many of the nurses had not realised the impact their behaviour was having on the organisation and their colleagues but there were also staff members who felt that talking to them about their absenteeism was 'picking' on them and this usually had a negative effect on management – employee relationships.

Conclusion

Although there has been some decrease in absence rates, no single strategy or combination of strategies has had a singnificant impact on absenteeism per se. Notwithstanding the disappointing results, it is our contention that the strategies were not in vain. A shared ownership of absenteeism and a collaborative approach to problem solving has facilitated improved cooperation and communication between management and staff. It is our belief that this improvement alone, while not tangibly measurable, has increased the ability of management to manage the effects of absenteeism more effectively since this study.

This article has been adapted and condensed from the article by G. William and K. Slater (1996), 'Absenteeism in nursing: A longitudinal study', *Asia Pacific Journal of Human Resources*, 34 (1): 111 – 21. Names and other details have been changed and report findings may have been given a different emphasis from the original. We are grateful to the authors and *Asia Pacific Journal of Human Resources* for allowing us to use the material in this way.

Questions 1 – 7

Do the following statements agree with the information given in Reading Passage 1?
In boxes 1 – 7 on your answer sheet write

> **YES**   *if the statement agrees with the information*
> **NO**   *if the statement contradicts the information*
> **NOT GIVEN** *if there is no information on this in the passage*

1. The prince William Hospital has been trying to reduce absenteeism amongst nurses for many years.

2. Nurses in the Prince William Hospital study believed that there were benefits in taking as little sick leave as possible.

3. Just over half the nurses in the 1986 study believed that management understood the effects that shift work had on them.

4. The Canadian study found that 'illness in the family' was a greater cause of absenteeism than 'work to do at home'.

5. In relation to management attitude to absenteeism the study at the Prince William Hospital found similar results to the two 1989 studies.

6. The study at the Prince William Hospital aimed to find out the causes of absenteeism amongst 250 nurses.

7. The study at the Prince William Hospital involved changes in management practices.

Complete the notes below.
Choose **ONE OR TWO WORDS** from the passage for each answer.
Write your answers in boxes 8 – 13 on your answer sheet.

In the first strategy, wards with the lowest absenteeism in different periods would win prizes donated by... **(8)** ...

In the second strategy, staff were given more control over their ... **(9)** ...

In the third strategy, nurses who appeared to be taking... **(10)** ...sick leave or... **(11)** ...were identified and counselled.

Initially, there was a... **(12)** ...per cent decrease in absenteeism.

The first strategy was considered ineffective and stopped. The second and third strategies generally resulted in better... **(13)** ...among staff.

You should spend about 20 minutes on *Questions 14 − 26 which are besed on Reading Passage 2 below*.

THE MOTOR CAR

A There are now over 700 million motor vehicles in the world − and the number is rising by more than 40 million each year. The average distance driven by car users is growing too − from 8 km a day per person in western Europe in 1965 to 25 km a day in 1995. This dependence on motor vehicles has given rise to major problems, including environmental pollution, depletion of oil resources, traffic congestion and safety.

B While emissions from new cars are far less harmful than they used to be, city streets and motorways are becoming more crowded than ever, often with older trucks, buses and taxis, which emit excessive levels of smoke and fumes. This concentration of vehicles makes air quality in urban areas unpleasant and sometimes dangerous to breathe. Even Moscow has joined the list of capitals afflicted by congestion and traffic fumes. In Mexico City, vehicle pollution is a major health hazard.

C Until a hundred years ago, most journeys were in the 20 km range, the distance conveniently accessible by horse. Heavy freight could only be carried by water or rail. The invention of the motor vehicle brought personal mobility to the masses and made rapid freight delivery possible over a much wider area. Today about 90 per cent of inland freight in the United Kingdom is carried by road. Clearly the world cannot revert to the horse-drawn wagon. Can it avoid being locked into congested and polluting ways of transporting people and goods?

D In Europe most cities are still designed for the old modes of transport. Adaptation to the motor car has involved adding ring roads, one-way systems and parking lots. In the United States, more land is assigned to car use than to housing. Urban sprawl means that life without a car is next to impossible. Mass use of motor vehicles has also killed or injured millions of people. Other social effects have been blamed on the car such as alienation and aggressive human behaviour.

E A 1993 study by the European Federation for Transport and Environment found that car transport is seven times as costly as rail travel in terms of the external social costs it entails such as congestion, accidents, pollution, loss of cropland and natural habitats, depletion of oil resources, and so on.

Yet cars easily surpass trains or buses as a flexible and convenient mode of personal transport. It is unrealistic to expect people to give up private cars in favour of mass transit.

F   Technical solutions can reduce the pollution problem and increase the fuel efficiency of engines. But fuel consumption and exhaust emissions depend on which cars are preferred by customers and how they are driven. Many people buy larger cars than they need for daily purposes or waste fuel by driving aggressively. Besides, global car use is increasing at a faster rate than the improvement in emissions and fuel efficiency which technology is now making possible.

G   One solution that has been put forward is the long-term solution of designing cities and neighbourhoods so that car journeys are not necessary – all essential services being located within walking distance or easily accessible by public transport. Not only would this save energy and cut carbon dioxide emissions, it would also enhance the quality of community life, putting the emphasis on people instead of cars. Good local government is already bringing this about in some places. But few democratic communities are blessed with the vision – and the capital – to make such profound changes in modern lifestyles.

H   A more likely scenario seems to be a combination of mass transit systems for travel into and around cities, with small 'low emission' cars for urban use and larger hybrid or lean burn cars for use elsewhere. Electronically tolled highways might be used to ensure that drivers pay charges geared to actual road use. Better integration of transport systems is also highly desirable—and made more feasible by modern computers. But these are solutions for countries which can afford them. In most developing countries, old cars and old technologies continue to predominate.

Questions 14 – 19

Reading Passage 2 has eight paragraphs (A – H). Which paragraphs concentrate on the following information? Write the appropriate letters (A – H) in boxes 14 – 19 on your answer sheet.

NB   *You need only write **ONE** letter for each answer.*

14. a comparison of past and present transportation methods
15. how driving habits contribute to road problems
16. the relative merits of cars and public transport
17. the writer's own prediction of future solutions
18. the increasing use of motor vehicles
19. the impact of the car on city development

Questions 20 – 26

Do the following statements agree with the information given in Reading Passage 2?
In boxes 20 – 26 on your answer sheet write

> **YES**   *if the statement agrees with the information*
> **NO**   *if the statement contradicts the information*
> **NOT GIVEN** *if there is no information on this in the passage*

20. Vehicle pollution is worse in European cities than anywhere else.

21. Transport by horse would be a useful alternative to motor vehicles.

22. Nowadays freight is not carried by water in the United Kingdom.

23. Most European cities were not designed for motor vehicles.

24. Technology alone cannot solve the problem of vehicle pollution.

25. People's choice of car and attitude to driving is a factor in the pollution problem.

26. Redesigning cities would be a short-term solution.

READING PASSAGE 3

You should spend about **20** *minutes on* **Questions** **27 – 40** *which are based on Reading Passage* **3** *on the following pages.*

Questions 27 – 33

Reading Passage 3 has eight paragraphs (**A – H**).

Choose the most suitable headings for paragraphs **B – H** *from the list of headings below. Write the appropriate numbers* (*i* – X) *in boxes 27 – 33 on your answer sheet.*

NB *There are more headings than paragraphs, so you will not use all of them.*

> **List of Headings**
>
> | | |
> |---|---|
> | i | Common objections |
> | ii | Who's planning what |
> | iii | This type sells best in the shops |
> | iv | The figures say it all |
> | v | Early trials |
> | vi | They can't get in without these |
> | vii | How does it work? |
> | viii | Fighting fraud |
> | ix | Systems to avoid |
> | x | Accepting the inevitable |

Example	*Answer*
Paragraph **A**	vi

27. Paragraph B
28. Paragraph C
29. Paragraph D
30. Paragraph E
31. Paragraph F
32. Paragraph G
33. Paragraph H

THE KEYLESS SOCIETY

A   Students who want to enter the University of Montreal's Athletic Complex need more than just a conventional ID card – their identities must be authenticated by an electronic hand scanner. In some California housing estates, a key alone is insufficient to get someone in the door; his or her voiceprint must also be verified, And soon, customers at some Japanese banks will have to present their faces for scanning before they can enter the building and withdraw their money.

B   All of these are applications of biometrics, a little-known but fast-growing technology that involves the use of physical or biological characteristics to identify individuals. In use for more than a decade at some high-security government institution in the United States and Canada, biometrics are now rapidly popping up in the everyday world. Already, more than 10,000 facilities, from prisons to day-care centres, monitor people's fingerprints or other physical parts to ensure that they are who they claim to be. Some 60 biometric companies around the world pulled in at least $ 22 million last year and that grand total is expected to mushroom to at least $ 50 million by 1999.

C   Biometric security systems operate by storing a digitised record of some unique human feature. When an authorised user wishes to enter or use the facility, the sysytem scans the person's corresponding characteristics and attempts to match them against those on record. Systems using fingerprints, hands, voices, irises, retinas and faces are already on the market. Others using typing patterns and even body odours are in various stages of development.

D   Fingerprint scanners are currently the most widely deployed type of biometric application, thanks to their growing use over the last 20 years by law-enforcement agencies. Sixteen American states now use biometric fingerprint verification systems to check that people claiming welfare payments are genuine. In June, politicians in Toronto voted to do the same, with a pilot project beginning next year.

E   To date, the most widely used commercial biometric system is the handkey, a type of hand scanner which reads the unique shape, size and irregularities of people's hands. Originally developed for nuclear power plants, the handkey received its big break when it was used to control access to the Olympic Village in Atlanta by more than 65,000 athletes, trainers and support staff. Now there are scores of other applications.

F Around the world, the market is growing rapidly. Malaysia, for example, is preparing to equip all of its airports with biometric face scanners to match passengers with luggage. And Japen's largest maker of cash dispensers is developing new machines that incorporate iris scanners. The first commercial biometric, a hand reader used by an American firm to monitor employee attendance, was introduced in 1974. But only in the past few years has the technology improved enough for the prices to drop sufficiently to make them commercially viable. 'When we started four years ago. I had to explain to everyone what a biometric is,' says one marketing expert. 'Now, there's much more awareness out there.'

G Not surprisingly, biometrics raise thorny questions bout privacy and the potential for abuse. Some worry that governments and industry will be tempted to use the technology to monitor individual behaviour. 'If someone used your fingerprints to match your health-insurance records with a credit-card record showing you regularly bought lots of cigarettes and fatty foods.' says one policy analyst, 'you would see your insurance payments go through the roof.' In Toronto, critics of the welfare fingerprint plan complained that it would stigmatise recipients by forcing them to submit to a procedure widely identified with criminals.

H Nonetheless, support for biometrics is growing in Toronto as it is in many other communities. In an increasingly crowded and complicated world, biometrics may well be a technology whose time has come.

Questions 34 – 40

Look at the following groups of people (***Questions 34 – 40***) *and the list of biometric systems* (**A – F**) *below.*

Match the groups of people to the biometric system associated with them in Reading Passage 3. Write the appropriate letters **A – F** *in boxes 34 – 40 on your answer sheet.*

NB   *You may use any biometric system more than once.*

34. sports students

35. Olympic athletes

36. airline passengers

37. welfare claimants

38. business employees

39. home owners

40. bank customers

List of Biometric Systems

(**A**) fingerprint scanner

(B) hand scanner

(C) body odour

(D) voiceprint

(E) face scanner

(F) typing pattern

WRITING TASK 1

You should spend about 20 minutes on this task.

The first chart below shows the results of a survey which sampled a cross-section of 100,000 people asking if they travelled abroad and why they travelled for the period 1994 – 98. The second chart shows their destinations over the same period.

Write a report for a university lecturer describing the information shown below.

You should write at least 150 words.

VISITS ABROAD BY UK RESIDENTS BY PURPOSE OF VISIT (1994 – 98)					
	1994	**1995**	**1996**	**1997**	**1998**
Holiday	15,246	14,898	17,896	19,703	20,700
Business	3,155	3,188	3,249	3,639	3,957
Visits to friends and relatives	2,689	2,628	2,774	3,051	3,181
Other reasons	982	896	1,030	1,054	990
TOTAL	**22,072**	**21,610**	**24,949**	**27,447**	**28,828**

DESTINATIONS OF VISITS ABROAD BY UK RESIDENTS BY MAIN REGION (1994 – 98)				
	Western Europe	**North America**	**Other areas**	**Total**
1994	19,371	919	1,782	**22,072**
1995	18,944	914	1,752	**21,610**
1996	21,877	1,167	1,905	**24,949**
1997	23,661	1,559	2,227	**27,447**
1998	24,519	1,823	2,486	**28,828**

WRITING TASK 2

You should write at least 250 words.

Without capital punishment (the death penalty) our lives are less secure and crimes of violence increase. Capital punishment is essential to control violence in society.

To what extent do you agree or disagree with this opinion?

You should write at least 250 words.

You should use your own ideas, knowledge and experience and support your arguments with examples and relevant evidence.

Task:

The candidate is to find out as much information as possible about an environmental group.

Candidate's cue card:

AN ENVIRONMENTAL GROUP

You are interested in joining a group of students at the university who work to protect the environment.

Ask the Examiner about:
the name of the proup
action that they take
the cost of membership
what members have to do
number of members
when the group was founded

Information for the Examiner:

the name of the group .... Green Action

action that they take .... planting trees, clearing up rubbish

the cost of membership .... $ 10 / £ 5 a year

what members have to do .... participate in two events (organised by the group) a year

number of members 4,500

when the group was founded 1996

Test 4

SECTION 1   Questions 1 - 10

Questions 1 and 2

Complete the notes below.

*Write **NO MORE THAN THREE WORDS** for each answer.*

MIC HOUSE AGENCY — REPAIRS

Example	*Answer*
Name:	Paul...SMILEY...

Address: Apartment 2, (**1**) ...., Newton

Length of lease: one year

Date moved in: (**2**) ....

Questions 3 - 9

Complete the table below.

Write A   if the repair will be done immediately.
　　　B   if the repair will be done during the following week.
　　　C   if the repair will be done in two or more weeks.

Item	Problem	When to be done
washing machine	leaking	Example **A**
cooker	(**3**)	(**4**) ....
windows	(5)	**B**
(**6**)	flickers	(**7**) ....
(**8**)	torn	(**9**) ....

Questions 10

*Write **NO MORE THAN THREE WORDS** or **A NUMBER** for each answer.*

workman to call between (**10**) .... and ....

SECTION 2   *Questions 11 − 20*

Questions 11 and 12

Circle the correct letters A − C.

11. At Rainforest Lodage there aren't any _____
    (A) telephones or TVs.
    (B) newspapers or TVs.
    (C) telephones or newspapers.

12. The guests are told to _____
    (A) carry their luggage to the cabin.
    (B) go straight to the restaurant.
    (C) wait an hour for dinner.

Questions 13 − 15

Complete the table below.
*Write **NO MORE THAN THREE WORDS** for each answer.*

TOUR NAME	DETAILS
Orchid and Fungi	walking tour
Four-Wheel-Dreve	tour to the (**13**) ....
Fishing	to catch lunch
Crocodile Cruise	departs at (**14**) .... daily
(**15**)	departs at sundown

Questions 16 - 20

Write **NO MORE THAN THREE WORDS** *for each answer*.

What **THREE** items of clothing does the speaker recommend for the rainforest?

16. ....

17. ....

18. ....

Which **TWO** things in the rainforest does the speaker give a warning about?

19. ....

20. ....

SECTION 3   *Questions 21 – 30*

Questions 21 – 25

Circle the correct letters A – C.

21. These sessions with a counsellor are _____
    (A) compulsory for all students.
    (B) available to any students.
    (C) for science students only.

22. The counsellor says that new students have to _____
    (A) spend more time on the college premises.
    (B) get used to working independently.
    (C) work harder than they did at school.

23. John complains that the resource centre _____
    (A) has limited opening hours.
    (B) has too few resources.
    (C) gets too crowded.

24. The counsellor suggests to John that _____
    (A) most other students can cope.
    (B) he needs to study all the time.
    (C) he should be able to fit in some leisure activities.

25. Before being able to help John the counsellor needs to _____
    (A) talk with some of his lecturers.
    (B) consult his tutor.
    (C) get more information from him.

Questions 26 – 30

Complete the notes below.

Write **NO MORE THAN THREE WORDS** *for each answer.*

WRITING

- Pay careful attention to the question
- Leave time to (**26**) ....

LISTENING

- Try to (**27**) .... lectures
- Check notes with (**28**) ....

READING

- Choose topics of (**29**) ....
- Buy a good (**30**) ....

SECTION 4   *Questions 31 – 40*

Questions 31 – 35

Circle the correct letters A – C.

31. John was first interested in the subject because of something _____
    (A) he had witnessed.
    (B) he had read about.
    (C) he had experienced.

32. The main research method was _____
    (A) interviews.
    (B) questionnaires.
    (C) observation.

33. Which pie chart shows the proportion of men and women respondents?

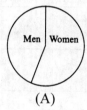 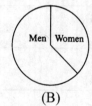 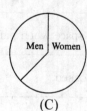

    (A)   (B)   (C)

34. How many respondents were there?
    (A) 50 – 100
    (B) 100 – 150
    (C) 150 – 200

35. The most common type of road rage incident involved _____
    (A) damage to property.
    (B) personal violence.
    (C) verbal abuse.

Questions 36 – 40

Which group gave the following advice?

Tick Column **A**   if it was mainly women.
Tick Column **B**   if it was mainly men.
Tick Column **C**   if it was both men and women.

	A	B	C
Example Don't stop to ask directions.	√		
(36) Avoid eye contact with other drivers.			
(37) Inform someone of your likely arrival time.			
(38) Ensure car keys are ready when you return to the car.			
(39) Leave plenty of space when parking.			
(40) Keep all doors locked.			

READING PASSAGE 1

*You should spend about **20** minutes on **Questions 1 – 13** which are based on Reading Passage 1 below.*

Green Wave Washes Over Mainstream Shopping

Research in Britain has shown that 'green consumers' continue to flourish as a significant group amongst shoppers. This suggests that politicians who claim environmentalism is yesterday's issue may be seriously misjudging the public mood.

A report from Mintel, the market research organisation, says that despite recession and financial pressures, more people than ever want to buy environmentally friendly products and a 'green wave' has swept through consumerism, taking in people previously untouched by environmental concerns, The recently published report also predicts that the process will repeat itself with 'ethical' concerns, involving issues such as fair trade with the Third World and the social record of businesses. Companies will have to be more honest and open in response to this mood.

Mintel's survey, based on nearly 1,000 consumers, found that the proportion who look for green products and are prepared to pay more for them has climbed from 53 per cent in 1990 to around 60 per cent in 1994. On average, they will pay 13 per cent more for such products, although this percentage is higher among women, managerial and professional groups and those aged 35 to 44.

Between 1990 and 1994 the proportion of consumers claiming to be unaware of or unconcerned about green issues fell from 18 to 10 per cent but the number of green spenders among older people and manual workers has risen substantially. Regions such as Scotland have also caught up with the south of England in their environmental concerns. According to Mintel, the image of green consumerism as associated in the past with the more eccentric members of society has virtually disappeared. The consumer research manager for Mintel, Angela Hughes, said it had become firmly established as a mainstream market. She explained that as far as the average person is concerned environmentalism has not 'gone off the boil'. In fact, it has spread across a much wider range of consumer groups, ages and occupations.

Mintel's 1994 survey found that 13 per cent of consumers are 'very dark green', nearly always buying environmentally friendly products, 28 per cent are 'dark green', trying 'as far as possible' to buy such products, and 21 per cent are 'pale green' – tending to

· 79 ·

buy green products if they see them. Another 26 per cent are 'armchair greens'; they said they care about environmental issues but their concern does not affect their spending habits. Only 10 per cent say they do not care about green issues.

Four in ten people are 'ethical spenders', buying goods which do not, for example, involve dealings with oppressive regimes. This figure is the same as in 1990, although the number of 'armchair ethicals' has risen from 28 to 35 per cent and only 22 per cent say they are unconcerned now, against 30 per cent in 1990. Hughes claims that in the twenty-first century, consumers will be encouraged to think more about the entire history of the products and services they buy, including the policies of the companies that provide them and that this will require a greater degree of honesty with consumers.

Among green consumers, animal testing is the top issue – 48 per cent said they would be deterred from buying a product if it had been tested on animals—followed by concerns regarding irresponsible selling, the ozone layer, river and sea pollution, forest destruction, recycling and factory farming. However, concern for specific issues is lower than in 1990, suggesting that many consumers feel that Government and business have taken on the environmental agenda.

Questions 1 – 6

Do the following statements agree with the claims of the writer of Reading Passage 1? In boxes 1 – 6 on your answer sheet write

YES　　　　*if the statement agrees with the claims of the writer*
NO　　　　*if the statement contradicts the claims of the writer*
NOT GIVEN *if it is impossible to say what the writer thinks about this*

1. The research findings report commercial rather than political trends.

2. Being financially better off has made shoppers more sensitive to buying 'green'.

3. The majority of shoppers are prepared to pay more for the benefit of the environment according to the research findings.

4. Consumers' green shopping habits are influenced by Mintel's findings.

5. Mintel have limited their investigation to professional and managerial groups.

6. Mintel undertakes mardet surveys on an annual basis.

Questions 7 – 9

*Chooose the appropriate letters **A** – **D** and write them in boxes 7 – 9 on your answer sheet.*

7. Politicians may have 'misjudged the public mood' because _____
   - (A) they are pre-occupied with the recession and financial problems.
   - (B) there is more widespread interest in the environment agenda than they anticipated.
   - (C) consumer spending has increased significantly as a result of 'green' pressure.
   - (D) shoppers are displeased with government policies on a range of issues.

8. What is Mintel?
   - (A) an environmentalist group
   - (B) a business survey organisation
   - (C) an academic research team
   - (D) a political organisation

9. A consumer expressing concern for environmental issues without actively supporting such principles is _____
   - (A) an 'ethical spender'.
   - (B) a 'very dark green' spender.
   - (C) an 'armchair green'.
   - (D) a 'pale green' spender.

Questions 10 − 13

Complete the summary using words from the box below.
Write your answers in boxes 10 − 13 on your answer sheet.

NB   *There are more answers than spaces, so you will not use them all.*

The Mintel report suggests that in future companies will be forced to practise greater... **(10)** ...in their dealings because of the increased awareness amongst ... **(11)** ...of ethical issues. This prediction is supported by the growth in the number of... **(12)** ...identified in the most recent survey published. As a consequence, it is felt that companies will have to think more carefully about their... **(13)** ...

environmental research	armchair ethicals
honesty and openness	environmentalists
ethical spenders	consumers
politicians	political beliefs
social awareness	financial constraints
social record	

READING PASSAGE 2

*You should spend about 20 minutes on **Questions 14 – 26** which are based on Reading Passage 2 below.*

A There is a great concern in Europe and North America about declining standards of literacy in schools. In Britain, the fact that 30 per cent of 16 year olds have a reading age of 14 or less has helped to prompt massive educational changes. The development of literacy has far-reaching effects on general intellectual development and thus anything which impedes the development of literacy is a serious matter for us all. So the hunt is on for the cause of the decline in literacy. The search so far has focused on socio-economic factors, or the effectiveness of 'traditional' versus 'modern' teaching techniques.

B The fruitless search for the cause of the increase in illiteracy is a tragic example of the saying 'They can't see the wood for the trees'. When teachers use picture books, they are simply continuing a long-established tradition that is accepted without question. And for the past two decades, illustrations in reading primers have become impoverished – sometimes to the point of extinction.

C Amazingly, there is virtually no empirical evidence to support the use of illustrations in teaching reading. On the contrary, a great deal of empirical evidence shows that pictures interfere in a damaging way with all aspects of learning to read. Despite this, from North America to the Antipodes, the first books that many school children receive are totally without text.

D A teacher's main concern is to help young beginner readers to develop not only the ability to recognise words, but the skills necessary to understand what these words mean. Even if a child is able to read aloud fluently, he or she may not be able to understand much of it: this is called 'barking at text'. The teacher's task of improving comprehension is made harder by influences outside the classroom. But the adverse effects of such things as television, video games, or limited language experiences at home, can be offset by experiencing 'rich' language at school.

E Instead, it is not unusual for a book of 30 or more pages to have only one sentence full of repetitive phrases. The artwork is often marvellous, but the pictures make the language redundant, and the children have no need to imagine anything when they read such books. Looking at a picture actively prevents children younger than nine from creating a mental image, and can make it difficult for older children. In order to learn how to comprehend, they need to practise making their own meaning in response to text. They need to have their innate powers of imagination trained.

F As they grow older, many children turn aside from books without pictures, and it is a situation made more serious as our culture becomes more visual. It is hard to wean children off picture books when pictures have played a major part throughout their formative reading experiences, and when there is competition for their attention from so many other sources of entertainment. The least intelligent are most vulnerable, but tests show that even intelligent children are being affected. The response of educators has been to extend the use of pictures in books and to simplify the language, even at senior levels. The Universities of Oxford and Cambridge recently held joint conferences to discuss the noticeably rapid decline in literacy among their undergraduates.

G Pictures are also used to help motivate children to read because they are beautiful and eye-catching. But motivation to read should be provided by listening to stories well read, where children imagine in response to the story. Then, as they start to read, they have this experience to help them understand the language. If we present pictures to save children the trouble of developing these creative skills, then I think we are making a great mistake.

H Academic journals ranging from educational research, psychology, language learning, psycholinguistics, and so on cite experiments which demonstrate how detrimental pictures are for beginner readers. Here is a brief selection:

I The research results of the Canadian educationalist Dale Willows were clear and consistent: pictures affected speed and accuracy and the closer the pictures were to the words, the slower and more inaccurate the child's reading became. She claims that when children come to a word they already know, then the pictures are unnecessary and distracting. If they do not know a word and look to the picture for a clue to its meaning, they may well be misled by aspects of the pictures which are not closely related to the meaning of the word they are trying to understand.

J Jay Samuels, an American psychologist, found that poor readers given no pictures learnt significantly more words than those learning to read with books with pictures. He examined the work of other researchers who had reported problems with the use of pictures and who found that a word without a picture was superior to a word plus a picture. When children were given words and pictures, those who seemed to ignore the pictures and pointed at the words learnt more words than the children who pointed at the pictures, but they still learnt fewer words than the children who had no illustrated stimuli at all.

Questions 14 − 17

Choose the appropriate letters **A** − **D** *and write them in boxes 14 − 17 on your answer sheet.*

14. Readers are said to 'bark' at a text when _____
    (A) they read too loudly.
    (B) there are too many repetitive words.
    (C) they are discouraged from using their imagination.
    (D) they have difficulty assessing its meaning.

15. The text suggests that _____
    (A) pictures in books should be less detailed.
    (B) picture can slow down reading progress.
    (C) picture books are best used with younger readers.
    (D) pictures make modern books too expensive.

16. University academics are concerned because _____
    (A) young people are showing less interest in higher education.
    (B) students cannot understand modern academic texts.
    (C) academic books are too childish for their undergraduates.
    (D) there has been a significant change in student literacy.

17. The youngest readers will quickly develop good reading skills if they _____
    (A) learn to associate the words in a text with pictures.
    (B) are exposed to modern teaching techniques.
    (C) are encouraged to ignore pictures in the text.
    (D) learn the art of telling stories.

Questions 18 - 21

Do the following statements agree with the information given in Reading Passage 2?
In boxes 18 - 21 on your answer sheet write

> **YES**   if the statement agrees with the information
> **NO**   if the statement contradicts the information
> **NOT GIVEN** if these is no information about this in the passage

18. It is traditionally accepted that children's books should contain few pictures.
19. Teachers aim to teach both word recognition and word meaning.
20. Older readers are having difficulty in adjusting to texts without pictures.
21. Literacy has improved as a result of recent academic conferences.

Questions 22 - 25

Reading Passage 2 has ten paragraphs, **A - J**. Which paragraphs state the following information?
Write the appropriate letters **A - J** in boxes 22 - 25 on your answer sheet.

NB   There are more paragraphs than summaries, so you will not use them all.

22. The decline of literacy is seen in groups of differing ages and abilities.
23. Reading methods currently in use go against research findings.
24. Readers able to ignore pictures are claimed to make greater progress.
25. Illustrations in books can give misleading information about word meaning.

Questions 26

From the list below choose the most suitable title for the whole of Reading Passage 2.
Write the appropriate letter **A - E** in box 26 on your answer sheet.

(A) The global decline in reading levels
(B) Concern about recent educational developments
(C) The harm that picture books can cause
(D) Research carried out on children's literature
(E) An examination of modern reading styles

IN SEARCH OF THE HOLY GRAIL

It has been called the Holy Grail of modern biology. Costing more than £2 billion, it is the most ambitious scientific project since the Apollo programme that landed a man on the moon. And it will take longer to accomplish than the lunar missions, for it will not be complete until early next century. Even before it is finished, according to those involved, this project should open up new understanding of, and new treatments for, many of the ailments that afflict humanity. As a result of the Human Genome Project, there will be new hope of liberation from the shadows of cancer, heart disease, autoimmune diseases such as rheumatoid arthritis, and some psychiatric illnesses.

The objective of the Human Genome Project is simple to state, but audacious in scope: to map and analyse every single gene within the double helix of humanity's DNA[1]. The project will reveal a new human anatomy – not the bones, muscles and sinews, but the complete genetic blueprint for a human being. Those working on the Human Genome Project claim that the new genetical anatomy will transform medicine and reduce human suffering in the twenty-first century. But others see the future through a darker glass, and fear that the project may open the door to a world peopled by Frankenstein's monsters and disfigured by a new eugenics[2].

The genetic inheritance a baby receives from its parents at the moment of conception fixes much of its later development, determining characteristics as varied as whether it will have blue eyes or suffer from a life-threatening illness such as cystic fibrosis. The human genome is the compendium of all these inherited genetic instructions. Written out along the double helix of DNA are the chemical letters of the genetic text. It is an extremely long text, for the human genome contains more than 3 billions letters. On the printed page it would fill about 7,000 volumes. Yet, within little more than a decade, the position of every letter and its relation to its neighbours will have been tracked down, analysed and recorded.

Considering how many letters there are in the human genome, nature is an excellent proof-reader. But sometimes there are mistakes. An error in a single 'word' – a gene – can give rise to the crippling condition of cystic fibrosis, the commonest genetic disorder among Caucasians. Errors in the genetic recipe for haemoglobin, the protein that gives blood its characteristic red colour and which carries oxygen from the lungs to the rest of the body, give rise to the most common single-gene disorder in the world: thalassaemia. More than 4,000 such single-gene defects are known to afflict humanity. The majority of them are fatal; the majority of the victims are children.

None of the single-gene disorders is a disease in the conventional sense, for which it would be possible to administer a curative drug: the defect is pre-programmed into every cell of the sufferer's body. But there is hope of progress. In 1986, American researchers identified the genetic defect underlying one type of muscular dystrophy. In 1989, a team of American and Canadian biologists announced that they had found the site of the gene which, when defective, gives rise to cystic fibrosis. Indeed, not only had they located the gene, they had analysed the sequence of letters within it and had identified the mistake responsible for the condition. At the least, these scientific advances may offer a way of screening parents who might be at risk of transmitting a single-gene defect to any children that they conceive. Foetuses can be texted while in the womb, and if found free of the genetic defect, the parents will be relieved of worry and stress, knowing that they will be delivered of a baby free from the disorder.

In the mid-1980s, the idea gained currency within the scientific world that the techniques which were successfully deciphering disorder-related genes could be applied to a larger project: if science can learn the genetic spelling of cystic fibrosis, why not attempt to find out how to spell 'human'? Momentum quickly built up behind the Human Genome Project and its objective of 'sequencing' the entire genome – writing out all the letters in their correct order.

But the consequences of the Human Genome Project go far beyond a narrow focus on disease. Some of its supporters have made claims of great extravagance – that the Project will bring us to understand, at the most fundamental level, what it is to be human. Yet many people are concerned that such an emphasis on humanity's genetic constitution may distort our sense of values, and lead us to forget that human life is more than just the expression of a genetic program written in the chemistry of DNA.

If properly applied, the new knowledge generated by the Human Genome Project may free humanity from the terrible scourge of diverse diseases. But if the new knowledge is not used wisely, it also holds the threat of creating new forms of discrimination and new methods of oppression. Many characteristics, such as height and intelligence, result not from the action of genes alone, but from subtle interactions between genes and the environment. What would be the implications if humanity were to understand, with precision, the genetic constitution which, given the same environment, will predispose one person towards a higher intelligence than another individual whose genes were differently shuffled?

Once before in this century, the relentless curiosity of scientific researchers brought to light forces of nature in the power of the atom, the mastery of which has shaped the destiny of nations and overshadowed all our lives. The Human Genome Project holds the promise that, ultimately, we may be able to alter our genetic inheritance if we so choose. But there is the central moral problem: how can we ensure that when we choose, we choose correctly? That such a potential is a promise and not a threat? We need only look at the past to understand the danger.

Glossary

[1] **DNA**   *Deoxyribonucleic acid, molecules responsible for the transference of genetic characteristics.*

[2] **eugenics**   *The science of improving the qualities of the human race, especially the careful selection of parents.*

Questions 27 – 32

Complete the sentences below (**Questions 27 – 32**) with words taken from Reading Passage 3.
Use **NO MORE THAN THREE WORDS OR A NUMBER** for each answer.
Write your answers in boxes 27 – 32 on your answer sheet.

Example	Answer
The passage compares the genetic instructions in DNA to	**chemical letters**

27. The passage compares the Project in scale to the ....

28. The possible completion date of the Project is ....

29. To write out the human genome on paper would require .... books.

30. A genetic problem cannot be treated with drugs because strictly speaking it is not a ....

31. Research into genetic defects had its first success in the discovery of the cause of one form of ....

32. The second success of research into genetic defects was to find the cause of ....

Questions 33 – 40

Classify the following statements as representing

    (A) *the writer's fears about the Human Genome Project*
    (B) *other people's fears about the Project reported by the writer*
    (C) *the writer's reporting of facts about the Project*
    (D) *the writer's reporting of the long-term hopes for the Project*

Write the appropriate letters **A – D** *in boxes 33 – 40 on your answer sheet.*

33. The Project will provide a new understanding of major diseases.

34. All the components which make up DNA are to be recorded and studied.

35. Genetic monsters may be created.

36. The correct order and inter-relation of all genetic data in all DNA will be mapped.

37. Parents will no longer worry about giving birth to defective offspring.

38. Being 'human' may be defined solely in terms of describable physical data.

39. People may be discriminated against in new ways.

40. From past experience humans may not use this new knowledge wisely.

WRITING

WRITING TASK 1

You should spend about 20 minutes on this task.

The table below shows the figures for imprisonment in five countries between 1930 and 1980.

Write a report for a university lecturer describing the information shown below.

You should write at least 150 words.

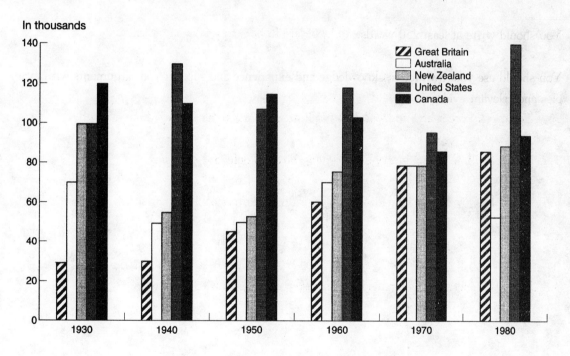

WRITING TASK 2

You should spend about 40 minutes on this task.

Present a written argument or case to an educated reader with no specialist knowledge of the following topic.

> *The position of women in society has changed markedly in the last twenty years. Many of the problems young people now experience, such as juvenile delinquency, arise from the fact that many married women now work and are not at home to care for their children.*
>
> *To what extent do you agree or disagree with this opinion?*

You should write at least 250 words.

You should use your own ideas, knowledge and experience and support your arguments with examples and relevant evidence.

Task:

The candidate is to find out as much information as possible about buying a book.

Candidate's cue card:

BUYING A BOOK

Your teacher recommended a good English language writing book to assist students with their written work.

Ask the examiner about: the level of the book
the title
the authors
the cost
place of purchase
extras — cassettes, answers

Information for the Examiner:

the level of the book .... It is valuable for students preparing for university entrance and fror advanced learners of English.

the title .... "Writing Academic English" or another text you know of

the authors .... by Walton and Hague

the cost .... around $ 40/£ 20

place of purchase .... Name a suitable bookshop in the town.

extras — cassettes, answers .... There is no cassette as it is only a writing book. It does not provide answers, but the teacher could help with corrections.

General Training : Reading and Writing Test A

SECTION 1   *Questions 1 – 13*

Questions 1 – 5

Look at the information on the following page about the use of vehicles in the University grounds.
In boxes 1 – 5 on your answer sheet write

> **TRUE**   *if the statement is true*
> **FALSE**   *if the statement is false*
> **NOT GIVEN**   *if the information is not given in the passage*

Example		*Answer*
The campus roads are not open to general members of the public.		**TRUE**

1. University employees do not need to pay for their parking permits.

2. Parking in Halls of Residence is handled by the Wardens of the Halls.

3. Having a University permit does not allow staff to park at Halls.

4. Parking permits cost £ 20 a year.

5. Students living in Hall do not need permission to park in Hall car parks.

USE OF UNIVERSITY GROUNDS
BY VEHICULAR TRAFFIC

The University grounds are private.

The University authorities only allow authorised members of the University, visitors and drivers of vehicles servicing the University to enter the grounds.

Members of staff who have paid the requisite fee and display the appropriate permit may bring a vehicle into the grounds. A University permit does not entitle them to park in Hall car parks however, unless authorised by the Warden of the Hall concerned.

Students may not bring vehicles into the grounds during the working day unless they have been given special permission by the Security Officer and have paid for and are displaying an appropriate entry permit. Students living in Halls of Residence must obtain permission from the Warden to keep a motor vehicle at their residence.

Students are reminded that if they park a motor vehicle on University premises without a valid permit, they will be fined £20.

Questions 6 – 13

Look at the patient information leaflet on the following page.

Match each of the following sentences with **TWO** possible endings **A** – **M** from the box below.

Write the appropriate letters **A** – **M** in boxes 6 – 13 on your answer sheet.

Example	*Answer*
Borodine tablets should not be given to...	**A and M**

Questions 6 and 7

Borodine tablets might be used to treat...

Questions 8 and 9

You must ask your doctor **before** taking Borodine tablets if you are already being treated for...

Questions 10 and 11

You do not need to consult your doctor immediately if Borodine tablets give you...

Questions 12 and 13

You must consult your doctor at once if you find Borodine tablets cause...

Possible Endings

(A) children under *12* years of age.

(B) a headache.

(C) an uncomfortable feeling in your stomach.

(D) symptoms similar to a cold.

(E) a change in your skin colour.

(F) anything treated by a prescription medicine.

(G) a kidney complaint.

(H) a whitening of the eyes.

(I) sore or broken skin.

(J) a fungal infection.

(K) a feeling of sadness.

(L) shortness of breath.

(M) a woman expecting a child.

The name of your medicine is
Borodine tablets.

WHAT ARE *Borodine* TABLETS USED FOR?

Borodine tablets are used to help relieve hay fever and conditions due to allergies, in particular skin reactions and a runny nose.

It is not recommended that *Borodine* tablets are given to children under 12 years of age or pregnant or breastfeeding women.

BEFORE YOU TAKE *Borodine* TABLETS

In some circumstances it is very important not to take *Borodine* tablets. If you ignore these instructions, this medicine could affect your heart rhythm.

Are you taking oral medicines for fungal infections?

Have you suffered a reaction to medicines containing *Borodine* before?

Do you suffer from any liver, kidney or heart disease?

If the answer to any of these questions is YES, do not take *Borodine* tablets before consulting your doctor.

AFTER TAKING *Borodine* TABLETS

Borodine tablets, like many other medicines, may cause side-effects in some people.

If you faint, stop taking *Borodine* tablets and tell your doctor immediately.

In addition *Borodine* tablets may cause problems with your vision, hair loss, depression or confusion, yellowing of your skin or your eyes.

If you have these effects whilst taking *Borodine* tablets, tell your doctor immediately.

Other side-effects are dizziness or headaches, and indigestion or stomachache. However, these effects are often mild and usually wear off after a few days' treatment. If they last for more than a few days, tell your doctor.

SECTION 2 Questions 14 – 20

Questions 14 – 20

Look at the introduction to *West Thames College* on the following page and at the statements (*Questions 14 – 20*) below.

In boxes 14 – 20 on your answer sheet write

TRUE	*if the statement is true*
FALSE	*if the statement is false*
NOT GIVEN	*if the information is not given in the passage*

14. Chiswick Polytechnic was closed at the same time West Thames College was opened.

15. Most of the students at the college come from outside the local area.

16. The college changed its name to West Thames College in 1993.

17. There are currently 6000 students over the age of 19 attending the college.

18. Students under the age of 16 cannot attend any of the courses offered by the college.

19. The college offers a more mature environment in which to learn than a school.

20. There are fewer subjects to study in the sixth form of a school than at the college.

WEST THAMES COLLEGE
BACKGROUND INFORMATION FOR CANDIDATES

West Thames College (initially known as Hounslow Borough College) came into existence in 1976 following the merger of Isleworth Polytechnic with part of Chiswick Polytechnic. Both parent colleges, in various guises, enjoyed a long tradition of service to the community dating back to the 1890s.

The college is located at London Road, Isleworth, on a site occupied by the Victorian house of the Pears family, Spring Grove House. An earlier house of the same name on this site had been the home of Sir Joseph Banks, the botanist who named Botany Bay with Captain Cook in 1770. Later he founded Kew Gardens.

Situated at the heart of West London, West Thames College is ideally placed to serve the training and education needs of local industry and local people. But its influence reaches much further than the immediate locality.

Under its former name, Hounslow Borough College, it had already established a regional, national and international reputation for excellence. In fact, about eight percent of its students come from continental Europe and further afield, whilst a further 52 percent are from outside the immediate area. Since 1 April 1993, when it became independent of the local authority and adopted its new title, West Thames College has continued to build on that first class reputation.

These days there is no such thing as a typical student. More than half of West Thames College's 6000 students are over 19 years old. Some of these will be attending college part-time under their employers' training schemes. Others will want to learn new skills purely out of interest, or out of a desire to improve their promotion chances, or they may want a change in career.

The college is also very popular with 16 – 18 year olds, who see it as a practical alternative to a further two years at school. They want to study in the more adult atmosphere the college provides. They can choose from a far wider range of subjects than it would be practical for a sixth form to offer. If they want to go straight into employment they can still study at college to gain qualifications relevant to the job, either on a day-release basis or through Network or the Modern Apprenticeship Scheme.

© *West Thames College 1996*

Questions 21 - 26

Look at the West Thames College's Services for Students on the following page. Each paragraph **A** - **H** *describes a different service provided by the college.*

From the list below (*i* - *xi*) *choose the most suitable summaries for paragraphs* **A**, **C** *and* **E** - **H**. *Write the appropriate numbers* (*i* - *xi*) *in boxes 21 - 26 on your answer sheet.*

NB   *There are more summaries than paragraphs, so you will not use them all.*

---

i	A shop for the books and stationery needed to study
ii	Counselling and welfare willing to listen, offer advice or arrange a referral
iii	An Examinations Office arranging exams and issuing certificates
iv	A Registrar's Office handling all fee payments and related enquiries
v	A Medical Service offering on-site assistance with health-related problems
vi	A tutorial system for regular one-to-one guidance, support and feedback
vii	Careers Advice helping students into employment
viii	An Admissions Service providing assistance in choosing and applying for higher education courses
ix	A Student Union representing students on college committees
x	Clubs and societies for students' free-time
xi	A Learning Support Service supporting students in studying, presenting information and handling numbers

---

21. Paragraph **A**

Example	*Answer*
Paragraph **B**	xi

22. Paragraph **C**

Example	*Answer*
Paragraph **D**	i

23. Paragraph **E**

24. Paragraph **F**

25. Paragraph **G**

26. Paragraph **H**

WEST THAMES COLLEGE SERVICES FOR STUDENTS

A

As a full-time student at West Thames College you will have your own Personal Mentor who will see you each week to guide you through your studies, and discuss any problems which may arise. We take a cooperative approach to the assessment of your work and encourage you to contribute to discussion.

B

This service provides specialist assistance and courses for those who need help to improve their writing, oral and numeracy skills for the successful completion of their college course. Help with basic skills is also available.

C

This service is available to anyone who is undecided as to which course to follow. It is very much a service for the individual, whatever your age, helping you to select the best option to suit your circumstances. The service includes educational advice, guidance and support, including a facility for accrediting your previous experience—the Accreditation of Prior Learning (APL). The Admissions Office is open Monday to Friday 9.00 am to 5.00 pm. All interviews are confidential and conducted in a relaxed and friendly atmosphere. Evening appointments are available on request.

D

The College Bookshop stocks a wide range of books, covering aspects of all courses, together with a good selection of stationery. It also supplies stamps, phone cards, blank videos and computer disks. The shop is open at times specified in the Student Handbook in the mornings, afternoons and evenings.

E

When students are weary from study and want the chance to relax and enjoy themselves with friends, they can participate in a number of recreational activities. Depending on demand, we offer a range of sporting activities including football, badminton, basketball, table tennis, volleyball, weight training and aerobics. For the non-sporting students we offer a debating society, video club, hair and beauty sessions, as well as a range of creative activities. Suggestions for activities from students are always welcome.

F

This confidential service is available if you have practical or personal difficulties during your course of study, whether of a financial or personal nature. Our Student Advisors can help you directly or put you in touch with someone else who can give you the help you need.

G

The College Nurses are there for general medical advice and for treatment of illness or injury. All visits are confidential. First aid boxes and fully-trained First Aiders are also on hand at various locations around the college.

H

West London employers have a permanent base in the centre of college, with access to a database of more than 24,000 jobs available locally and in Central London. They will also help you with job applications and interview techniques.

© *West Thames College 1996*

Read the following passage and answer Questions 27 – 40.

The Discovery of Uranus

Someone once put forward an attractive though unlikely theory. Throughout the Earth's annual revolution around the sun there is one point of space always hidden from our eyes. This point is the opposite part of the Earth's orbit, which is always hidden by the sun. Could there be another planet there, essentially similar to our own, but always invisible?

If a space probe today sent back evidence that such a world existed it would cause not much more sensation than Sir William Herschel's discovery of a new planet, Uranus, in 1781.

Herschel was an extraordinary man—no other astronomer has ever covered so vast a field of work—and his career deserves study. He was born in Hanover in Germany in 1738, left the German army in 1757, and arrived in England the same year with no money but quite exceptional music ability. He played the violin and oboe and at one time was organist in the Octagon Chapel in the city of Bath. Herschel's was an active mind, and deep inside he was con-

scious that music was not his destiny; he therefore read widely in science and the arts, but not until 1772 did he come across a book on astronomy. He was then 34, middle-aged by the standards of the time, but without hesitation he embarked on his new career, financing it by his professional work as a musician. He spent years mastering the art of telescope construction, and even by present-day standards his instruments are comparable with the best.

Serious observation began in 1774. He set himself the

astonishing task of 'reviewing the heavens', in other words, pointing his telescope to every accessible part of the sky and recording what he saw. The first review was made in 1775; the second, and most momentous, in 1780 – 1781. It was during the latter part of this that he discovered Uranus. Afterwards, supported by the royal grant in recognition of his work, he was able to devote himself entirely to astronomy. His final achievements spread from the sun and moon to remote galaxies (of which he discovered hundreds), and papers flooded from his pen until his death in 1822.

Among these there was one sent to the Royal Society in 1781, entitled *An Account of a Comet*. In his own words:

On Tuesday the 13th of March, between ten and eleven in the evening , while I was examining the small stars in the neighbourhood of H Geminorum, I perceived one that appeared visibly larger than the rest; being struck with its uncommon magnitude, I compared it to H Geminorum and the small star in the quartile between Auriga and Gemini, and finding it to be much larger than either of them, suspected it to be a comet.

Herschel's care was the hallmark of a great observer; he was not prepared to jump to any conclusions. Also, to be fair, the discovery of a new planet was the last thought in anybody's mind. But further observation by other astronomers besides Herschel revealed two curious facts. For a comet, it showed a remarkably sharp disc; furthermore, it was moving so slowly that it was thought to be a great distance from the sun, and comets are only normally visible in the immediate vicinity of the sun. As its orbit came to be worked out the truth dawned that it was a new planet far beyond Saturn's realm, and that the 'reviewer of the heavens' had stumbled across an unprecedented prize. Herschel wanted to call it georgium sidus (Star of George) in honour of his royal patron King George III of Great Britain. The planet was later for a time called Herschel in honour of its discoverer. The name Uranus, which was first proposed by the German astronomer Johann Elert Bode, was in use by the late 19th century.

Uranus is a giant in construction, but not so much in size; its diameter compares unfavourably with that of Jupiter and Saturn, though on the terrestrial scale it is still colossal. Uranus' atmosphere consists largely of hydrogen and helium, with a trace of methane. Through a telescope the planet appears as a small bluish-green disc with a faint green periphery. In 1977, while recording the occultation[1] of a star behind the planet, the American astronomer James L. Elliot discovered the presence of five rings encircling the equator of Uranus. Four more rings were discovered in January 1986 during the exploratory flight of *Voyager 2*[2]. In addition to its rings, Uranus has 15 satellites ('moons'), the last 10 discovered by *Voyager 2* on the same flight; all revolve about its equator and move with the planet in an east-west direction. The two largest moons, Titania and Oberon, were discovered by Herschel in 1787. The next two, Umbriel and Ariel, were found in 1851 by the British astronomer William Lassell. Miranda, thought before 1986 to be the innermost moon, was discovered in 1948 by the American astronomer Gerard Peter Kuiper.

Glossary:

[1]occultation   in astronomy, when one object passes in front of another and hides the second from view, especially, for example, when the moon comes between an observer and a star or planet

[2]*Voyager 2*   an unmanned spacecraft sent on a voyage past Saturn, Uranus and Jupiter in 1986, during which it sent back information about these planets to scientists on earth

Questions 27 – 31

Complete the table below.
Write a date for each answer.
Write your answers in boxes 27 – 31 on your answer sheet.

Event	Date
Example William Herschel was born	*Answer* **1738**
Herschel began investigating astronomy	**(27)** ....
Discovery of the planet Uranus	**(28)** ....
Discovery of the moons Titania and Oberon	**(29)** ....
First discovery of Uranus' rings	**(30)** ....
Discovery of the last 10 moons of Uranus	**(31)** ....

Questions 32 – 36

Do the following statements reflect the claims of the writer of the Reading Passage?

In boxes 32 – 36 on your answer sheet write

YES	*if the statement reflects the claims of the writer*
NO	*if the statement contradicts the writer*
NOT GIVEN	*if it is impossible to say what the writer thinks about this*

Example	*Answer*
Herschel was multi-talented.	**YES**

32. It is improbable that there is a planet hidden behind the sun.

33. Herschel knew immediately that he had found a new planet.

34. Herschel collaborated with other astronomers of his time.

35. Herschel's newly-discovered object was considered to be too far from the sun to be a comet.

36. Herschel's discovery was the most important find of the last three hundred years.

Questions 37 – 40

*Complete each of the following statements (**Questions 37 – 40**) with a name from the Reading passage.*

Write your answers in boxes 37 – 40 on your answer sheet.

The suggested names of the new planet started with ... (**37**) ..., then... (**38**) ..., before finally settling on Uranus.

The first five rings around Uranus were discovered by... (**39**) ....

From 1948 until 1986, the moon... (**40**) ...was believed to be the moon closest to the surface of Uranus.

WRITING

WRITING TASK 1

You should spend no more than 20 minutes on this task.

> *You borrowed some books from your school or college library. Unfortunately you have to go away to visit a sick relative and cannot return the books in time.*
>
> *Write a letter to the library. Explain what has happened and tell them what you want to do about it.*

You should write at least 150 words.

You do **NOT** need to write your own address.

Begin your letter as follows:

Dear _____,

WRITING TASK 2

You should spend no more than 40 minutes on this task.

As part of a class assignment you have to write about the following topic.

> *Some governments say how many children a family can have in their country. They may control the number of children someone has through taxes.*
>
> *It is sometimes necessary and right for a government to control the population in this way.*
>
> *Do you agree or disagree?*
>
> *Give reasons for your answer.*

You should write at least 250 words.

General Training: Reading and Writing Test B

SECTION 1   Questions 1 – 13

Questions 1 – 7

Look at the three restaurant advertisements on the following page.
Answer the questions below by writing the letters of the appropriate restaurants (A – C) in boxes 1 – 7 on your answer sheet.

Example	*Answer*
It stops serving lunch at 2.30 pm.	**B**

1. It is open for breakfast.

2. It is open every night for dinner.

3. It is only open for lunch on weekdays.

4. It has recently returned to its previous location.

5. It welcomes families.

6. It caters for large groups.

7. It only opens at weekends.

DINING OUT

A

Aboyne
The original
Luigi's
Italian Restaurant
is now back in Aboyne

**231 Beach Road,
Aboyne**

(ample parking available)

Open:
Luncheon 12 to 3 pm
Dinner 6 to 10 pm

TUESDAY TO SUNDAY

Entrees $5.50   Mains $8.00
Free ice cream for the kids

Special functions
Up to 120 people

Reservations: Phone 9763 3501

B

Mermaids

Italian & Seafood Cuisine

Lunch:
Tuesday – Friday
12 noon – 2.30 pm

Dinner:
7 nights
6.00 pm – 11.30 pm

Tel & Fax: 9784 1234

**54 Shore Street
Kempton**

C

RIVIERA
CRUISING BOAT CLUB

Breakfast by the water
$5.00

Saturday & Sunday
8.00 am to 11.00 am

- Australian
- Continental
- American

**At Riviera
Cruising Boat Club
9753 5544
The Quay, Gateside**

Questions 8 – 13

Read the information given in ' New Electricity Account Payment Facilities' on the following page and look at the statements below (**Questions 8 – 13**).

In boxes 8 – 13 on your answer sheet write

TRUE	if the statement is true
FALSE	if the statement is false
NOT GIVEN	if the information is not given in the passage

Example	Answer
You must pay your account by mail.	**FALSE**

8 . If you want a receipt, you should send your payment to the Southport address.

9.   You may pay your account at branches of the Federal Bank.

10. You must pay the full amount, instalments are not permitted.

11. The Coastside Power Office is open on Saturday mornings.

12. You may pay your account by phone using your credit card.

13. There is a reduction for prompt payment.

NEW ELECTRICITY ACCOUNT PAYMENT FACILITIES

AVAILABLE FROM 1 JULY 1998

After 1 July 1998, you may pay your electricity account in any of the following ways:

1. Payments via mail:
    (A) No receipt required:
        Mail payments to:

    > Coastside Power
    > Locked Bag 2760
    > Southport NSW 3479

    (B) Receipt required:
        Mail payments to:

    > Coastside Power
    > PO Box 560
    > Northbridge NSW 3472

2. Agency payments (payments directly to the bank):
    Payments can be made at any branch of the Federal Bank by completing the deposit slip attached to your account notice.
    NB: This facility is no longer available at South Pacific Bank branches.

3. Payments directly to Coastside Power Office:
    Payments can be made directly to Coastside Power Office at 78 – 80 Third Avenue, Northbridge. Office hours are Monday to Friday, 8.30 am to 4.30 pm.

Payment may be by personal cheque, bank cheque or cash.

Note: Payments cannot be made by phone.

SECTION 2   *Questions 14 – 26*

Questions 14 – 20

Read the passage about personal computers on the following page and look at the statements below (*Questions 14 – 20*).

In boxes 14 – 20 on your answer sheet write

TRUE	*if the statement is true*
FALSE	*if the statement is false*
NOT GIVEN	*if the information is not given in the passage*

14. There are two computers and two printers available for public use at the library.

15. You can buy floppy disks at the information desk.

16. The information desk is closed at weekends.

17. It is essential to reserve a computer three days in advance if you want to use one.

18. If you are more than a quarter of an hour late, you could lose your reservation for the computer.

19. Library employees do not have detailed knowledge of computers.

20. The library runs courses for people who want to learn about computers.

Central Library

PERSONAL COMPUTERS AVAILABLE FOR PUBLIC TO USE

- 2 personal computers are available, for a fee of $ 5.00. There is also an ink jet printer attached to each terminal. The library has a number of commercially available programs for word processing and spreadsheets.

- A4 paper can be bought from the desk if you wish to print your work. Alternatively you can bring your own paper. If you wish to store information however, you will need to bring your own floppy disk.

Bookings

Because of high demand, a maximum of one hour's use per person per day is permitted. Bookings may be made up to three days in advance. Bookings may be made in person at the information desk or by phoning 8673 8901 during normal office hours. If for some reason you cannot keep your appointment, please telephone. If the library is not notified and you are 15 minutes late, your time can be given to someone else. Please sign in the visitors' book at the information desk when you first arrive to use the computer.

Please note that staff are not available to train people or give a lot of detailed instruction on how to use the programs. Prior knowledge is, therefore, necessary. However, tutorial groups are available for some of the programs and classes are offered on a regular basis. Please see the loans desk for more information about our computer courses.

Questions 21 – 26

The text on *Atlas English Language College* on the following page has seven paragraphs (**A** – **G**).
Choose the most suitable headings for paragraphs **B** – **G** from the list of headings below.
Write the appropriate numbers (*i* – *ix*) in boxes 21 – 26 on your answer sheet.

NB There are more headings than paragraphs, so you will not use all of them.

```
                    List of Headings
    i     Recognition of your achievements
    ii    Courses start every week
    iii   Other services/Pastoral care/Personal arrangements
    iv    A personal approach
    v     Two meals every day
    vi    First-class staff
    vii   Up-to-date classroom practice
    viii  Discovering a new language
    ix    Monitored achievement
```

Example	*Answer*
Paragraph **A**	ii

21. Paragraph **B**

22. Paragraph **C**

23. Paragraph **D**

24. Paragraph **E**

25. Paragraph **F**

26. Paragraph **G**

GOOD REASONS FOR CHOOSING
ATLAS ENGLISH LANGUAGE COLLEGE

On an English course with Atlas English Language College, you improve your language skills and make friends from all over the world!

A Because Atlas courses start every Monday of the year, there's bound to be one that fits in with your academic, personal or professional commitments. Whatever your level of language ability, from beginner to advanced, you can choose to study for any length of time, from two weeks to a full year. Courses match a range of individual requirements, from intensive examination preparation to short summer programmes. Most courses commence at 9 am and run till 3 pm.

B If you take an intensive full-time course, we will help you to select the Special Interest Options which best suit your goals. From then on, our teacher will discuss your work with you on a weekly basis. This means that you should develop the language skills you need—and that you are helped to study at your own pace.

C The popularity and success of any language school depend greatly on the quality of the teachers and the methods they employ. All Atlas teachers have specialist qualifications in the teaching of English to foreign students and are all native speakers. We employ only experienced professionals with a proven record of success in the classroom.

D Atlas's teaching methodology is constantly revised as more is discovered about the process of learning a new language. Our teachers have access to an extensive range of materials, including the very latest in language teaching technology.

E On your first day at school, you will take a test which enables our Director of Studies to place you at the appropriate study level. Your progress will be continuously assessed and , once you have achieved specific linguistic goals, you will move up to a higher level of study.

F Every Atlas course fee includes accommodation in carefully selected homestay families. Breakfast and dinner each day are also included, so you need have no concerns about having to look for somewhere to live once you get to the school.

G On completion of any Intensive, Examination or Summer course, you will receive the Atlas Course Certificate of Attendance. On completion of a four-week course or longer you will also receive the Atlas Academic Record that reflects your ability in every aspect of the language from conversation to writing. Such a record will allow you to present your linguistic credentials to academic institutions or potential employers around the world.

adapted with permission from a brochure published by EF Education

SECTION 3   *Questions 27 - 40*

Questions 27 - 32

The Reading Passage on the following pages has seven paragraphs (**A - G**).

Choose the most suitable headings for paragraphs **A - B** and **D - G** from the list of headings below.

Write the appropriate numbers (*i - ix*) in boxes 27 - 32 on your answer sheet.

NB   *There are more headings than paragraphs, so you will not use all of them.*

List of Headings

i	Robots working together
ii	Preparing LGVs for take-over
iii	Looking ahead
iv	The LGVs' main functions
v	Split location for newspaper production
vi	Newspapers superseded by technology
vii	Getting the newspaper to the printing centre
viii	Controlling the robots
ix	Beware of robots!

Example	*Answer*
Paragraph C	ix

27. Paragraph **A**

28. Paragraph **B**

29. Paragraph **D**

30. Paragraph **E**

31. Paragraph **F**

32. Paragraph **G**

ROBOTS AT WORK

A

The newspaper production process has come a long way from the old days when the paper was written, edited, typeset and ultimately printed in one building with the journalists working on the upper floors and the printing presses going on the ground floor. These days the editor, sub-editors and journalists who put the paper together are likely to find themselves in a totally different building or maybe even in a different city. This is the situation which now prevails in Sydney. The daily paper is compiled at the editorial headquarters, known as the pre-press centre, in the heart of the city but printed far away in the suburbs at the printing centre. Here human beings are in the minority as much of the work is done by automated machines controlled by computers.

B

Once the finished newspaper has been created for the next morning's edition, all the pages are transmitted electronically from the pre-press centre to the printing centre. The system of transmission is an update on the sophisticated page facsimile system already in use on many other newspapers. An image-setter at the printing centre delivers the pages as film. Each page takes less than a minute to produce, although for colour pages four versions are used, one each for black, cyan, magenta and yellow. The pages are then processed into photographic negatives and the film is used to produce aluminium printing plates ready for the presses.

C

A procession of automated vehicles is busy at the new printing centre where the Sydney Morning Herald is printed each day. With lights flashing and warning horns honking, the robots (to give them their correct name, the LGVs or laser-guided vehicles) look for all the world like enthusiastic machines from a science-fiction movie, as they follow their own random paths around the plant busily getting on with their jobs. Automation of this kind is now standard in all modern newspaper plants. The robots can detect unauthorised personnel and alert security staff immediately if they find an 'intruder' and not surprisingly, tall tales are already being told about the machines starting to take on personalities of their own.

D

The robots' principle job, however, is to shift the newsprint (the printing paper) that arrives at the plant in huge reels and emerges at the other end some time later as newspapers. Once the size of the day's paper and the publishing order are determined at head office, the information is punched into the computer and the LGVs are programmed to go about their work. The LGVs collect the appropriate size paper reels and take them where they have to go. When the press needs another reel its computer alerts the LGV system. The Sydney LGVs move busily around the press room fulfilling their two key functions—to collect reels of newsprint either from the reel stripping stations or from the racked supplies in the newsprint storage area. At the stripping station the tough wrapping that helps to protect a reel of paper from rough handling is removed. Any damaged paper is peeled off and the reel is then weighed.

E

Then one of the four paster robots moves in. Specifically designed for the job, it trims the paper neatly and prepares the reel for the press. If required, the reel can be loaded directly onto the press. If not needed immediately, an LGV takes it to the storage area. When the press computer calls for a reel, an LGV takes it to the reel-loading area of the presses. It lifts the reel onto the loading position and places it in the correct spot with complete accuracy. As each reel is used up, the press drops the heavy cardboard core into a waste bin, and when the bin is full, another LGV collects it and deposits the cores into a shredder for recycling.

F

The LGVs move at walking speed. Should anyone step in front of one or get too close, sensors stop the vehicle until the path is clear. The company has chosen a laser-guide function system for the vehicles because, as the project development manager says, 'The beauty of it is that if you want to change the routes, you can work out a new route on your computer and lay it down for them to follow.' When an LGV's batteries run low, it will take itself off line and go to the nearest battery maintenance point for replacement batteries. And all this is achieved with absolute minimum human input and a much reduced risk of injury to people working in the printing centres.

G

The question newspaper workers must now ask, however is, how long will it be before the robots are writing the newspapers as well as running the printing centre, churning out the latest edition every morning?

Questions 33 – 40

Using the information in the passage, complete the flow chart below.
Write your answers in boxes 33 – 40 on your answer sheet.
Use **NO MORE THAN THREE WORDS** *from the passage for each answer.*

The Production Process

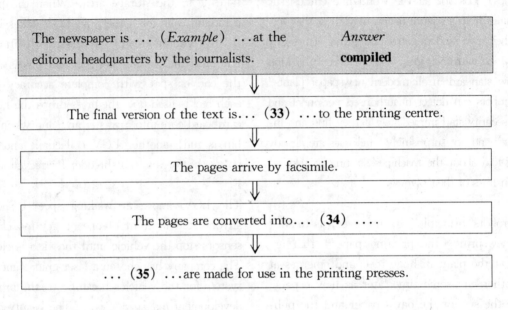

The newspaper is ... (*Example*) ...at the editorial headquarters by the journalists.

Answer
compiled

↓

The final version of the text is... (**33**) ...to the printing centre.

↓

The pages arrive by facsimile.

↓

The pages are converted into... (**34**) ....

↓

... (**35**) ...are made for use in the printing presses.

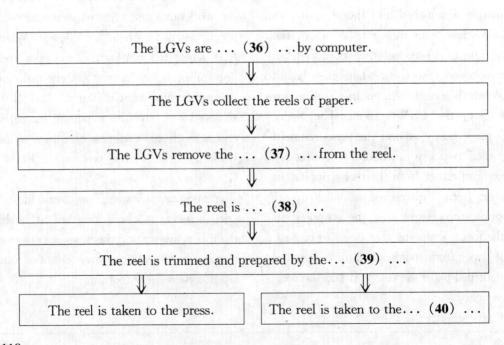

The LGVs are ... (**36**) ...by computer.

↓

The LGVs collect the reels of paper.

↓

The LGVs remove the ... (**37**) ...from the reel.

↓

The reel is ... (**38**) ...

↓

The reel is trimmed and prepared by the... (**39**) ...

↓   ↓

The reel is taken to the press.   The reel is taken to the... (**40**) ...

WRITING

WRITING TASK 1

You should spend no more than 20 minutes on this task.

> *You travelled by plane last week and your suitcase was lost.*
> *You have still heard nothing from the airline company.*
>
> *Write to the airline and explain what happened. Describe your suitcase and tell them what was in it. Find out what they are going to do about it.*

You should write at least 150 words.

You do **NOT** need to write your own address.

Begin your letter as follows:

Dear _____ ,

WRITING TASK 2

You should spend no more than 40 minutes on this task.

As part of a class assignment you have to write about the following topic.

> *Millions of people every year move to English-speaking countries such as Australia, Britain or America, in order to study at school, college or university.*
>
> *Why do so many people want to study in English?*
> *Why is English such an important international language?*
>
> *Give reasons for your answer.*

You should write at least 250 words.

Tapescripts

SECTION 1

LOUISE	Oh hello, I'd like to join the video library.
MR MAX	OK. Would you like to fill in the application form now?
LOUISE	Yes, I can do it now.
MR MAX	Hold on and I'll get a form. Now, I'll just ask you a few questions and then I'll get you to sign at the bottom.
LOUISE	Right.
MR MAX	What's your full name?
LOUISE	Louise Cynthia Jones.
MR MAX	Jones?
LOUISE	Yes, that's right.
Repeat	
MR MAX	OK, and what's your address?
LOUISE	Apartment 1, 72 Black Street, Highbridge.
MR MAX	Black Street, that's just around the corner, isn't it?
LOUISE	Yes.
MR MAX	OK, so the post code is 2085, right?
LOUISE	Yes, 2085.
MR MAX	Mm. And your telephone number? I need both home and work.
LOUISE	Home is 9835 6712 and work is 9456 1309. Do you need any ID or anything like that?
MR MAX	Yes, we need your driver's licence number, that is if you have one.
LOUISE	Yes, I know if off by heart, it's an easy one, 2020BD. Do you need to see it?
MR MAX	Yes, I'm afraid I do.
LOUISE	Mm...here.
MR MAX	Right, thanks. And could you tell me your date of birth please?
LOUISE	25 July 1977.
MR MAX	That's the most important part out of the way, but could I just ask you a few questions for a survey we're conducting?
LOUISE	OK.

Example

Q1

Q2

Q3

Q4

Q5

MR MAX	What kind of videos do you prefer to watch? Have a look at this list.
LOUISE	Well, <u>I love anything that makes me laugh. I just love to hear jokes and funny punch lines.</u> I'm not very keen on westerns, although my father likes them, but I'm a real softie, so <u>anything with a bit of a love story is good for me.</u> It doesn't matter how old. Not musicals though, they're too much!
MR MAX	Anything else?
LOUISE	I'm completely taken by <u>documentaries of the great outdoors, you know the sort, animals, plants and faraway places.</u> I saw wonderful one on dolphins last week. It was amazing.
MR MAX	Now, I think that's all from me, except I need you to sign here on the line. Here's a pen. Oh, and I nearly forgot, the membership fee. <u>$25, refundable</u> if you leave the library for any reason.
LOUISE	There you are. And do I sign here?
MR MAX	Yes, that's it. You can borrow videos now, if you like, but <u>your card won't be ready until next week</u>. You can come and pick it up when you bring your first videos back. That is if you want to take some now.
LOUISE	Yes, I'd like to. I'll have a look around.
MR MAX	Fine.

Q6 · Q7 · Q8 · Q9 · Q10

SECTION 2

INTERVIEWER	A dream came true in 1995, when over 96 days of the spring and summer, and expedition of four men undertook what they believe to have been the first and only complete end-to-end crossing of Morocco's Attora mountains. I talked to Charles Owen, the leader or the expedition group, about the trip. Charles, how much planning went on beforehand?
CHARLES	Well, as you know, I run these walking trips across the mountains for tourists and over the years, I've collected maps and other data to <u>prepare what I call a 'route book'</u> for this trip and this book basically shows the route across the mountains that we took.
INTERVIEWER	You actually broke records while you were out there, didn't you?
CHARLES	Mmm. Yes, <u>it was 900 miles in total</u> and we managed to climb 32 peaks that were over 3000 metres high, including *Toubkal*, <u>which is of course the highest in North Africa.</u> We weren't actually out to make a name for ourselves—it just happened really.

Q11 · Q12 · Q13

INTERVIEWER	What was the weather like?	
CHARLES	It got us right from day one and <u>we were pretty taken aback really</u>	*Q14*
	<u>to find that it rained on quite a number of days,</u> and so we were	
	forced to start re-planning our route almost from the outset. One	
	of the obvious problems is the heavy snow which blocks the moun-	
	tain passes, so you have to make considerable detours. When we	
	were on the way to Imilchil, for example, the snow forced us into	
	a northern bypass which was new to us, but anyway, either way	
	we would have been rewarded because we fell upon amazing, high	
	meadows, huge gorges and wonderful snow-capped mountains.	
	The scenery was as fine as any we saw on the trip and that was	
	how it was every time—<u>having to take another pass was never a</u>	*Q15*
	<u>disappointment.</u>	

INTERVIEWER	It was in many ways a social trip, wasn't it?	
CHARLES	Yes, yes...we'd arranged to meet up with friends at various points	
	on the journey. I mean this was actually one of the purposes of the	
	trip...and <u>we managed to keep all these dates,</u> which is amazing	*Q16*
	really considering the detours we made. <u>An old friend acted as a</u>	*Q17*
	<u>sort of transport organiser</u> for everyone and the Hotel Ali in Mar-	
	rakech was a good social base—I'd really recommend it, although	
	I can't remember who runs it. Anyway, <u>groups of friends actual-</u>	*Q18*
	<u>ly joined us for three-week stints</u> and others just linked up with	
	us. Some, whom we hadn't met before the trip at all, tagged on	
	for short bursts—people from the area—who just came along for	
	the tide. But outside the major visitor areas like Toubkal we only	
	met one other group of travellers like ourselves in the whole 96	
	days.	
INTERVIEWER	Were there any bad moments?	
CHARLES	We took two, I must say, long-suffering donkeys with us to help	
	transport water and tents and things. I suppose if we were to do it	
	all again we'd probably hire donkeys along the way. <u>Taza and</u>	*Q19*
	<u>Tamri, as we called them after the last places in the trip,</u> well,	
	they made quite a unique journey between them, and...but it was	
	continuously demanding for them. On both the really high sum-	
	mits, <u>they took diversions that were quite out of character</u> and I	*Q20*
	can only assume that it must have been due to tiredness.	
INTERVIEWER	Well, thank you...And Charles has put together a video about	

this journey and continues to lead groups to the Attora mountains, so if you want further information...

SECTION 3

JANE Hi Tim! (Tim: Jane.) How are you? (Tim : Fine.) I'd been wondering when I'd run into you. Have you been here long?

TIM I arrived yesterday, on Sunday. How about you?

JANE I got here a few days ago, on Saturday. No—wait a minute, what's today? —Sorry <u>Friday</u>, not Saturday.   *Q21*

TIM But we didn't have to be here till today.

JANE Yes, I know, but I wanted to get my things moved into my room, and just take a look around. So, did you decide to do English in the end?

TIM No, I changed my mind and opted for history instead. <u>And you're doing biology, if I remember correctly.</u>   *Q22*

JANE <u>Yes</u>, although to start with I couldn't decide between that and geography.

TIM How much reading have you got? I was given an amazingly long list of books to read. See!

JANE Wow, it does look pretty long.

TIM Well, <u>I counted 57.</u> I could hardly believe it! What's your list like?   *Q23*

JANE Well, it's not as long as yours, but it's sitll pretty big. <u>There are 43.</u> I don't   *Q24* know how I'm going to get through them all.

TIM Well you don't have to read them all this week! You just have to stay ahead of the lectures and seminars. Have you got your class schedule yet?

JANE Yep. It came with the reading list. When's your first lecture?

TIM <u>Tuesday. How about you?</u>

JANE <u>The day after.</u> It's my busiest day; I've got two lectures in the morning and   *Q25* one in the afternoon.

JANE It's going to be different from school, isn't it!

TIM Yeah, particularly the lectures. Have you got any special strategy for listening to lectures?

JANE Well <u>I'm going to use a cassette recorder and record them all.</u>   *Q26*

TIM What! Are you allowed to?

JANE Sure. Lots of people do it nowadays. It means you can listen to the lectures all over again later, and make really good notes.

TIM I couldn't do that. I like to take notes as I'm listening. I usually find I get all the important points. Reading is different of course. <u>My approach is to skim</u>   *Q27* <u>the book first</u> to see what's important and what isn't. It saves hours of time.

JANE But what if you miss something?

TIM You don't mean you're going to read every word, do you?

JANE Well, that's what I usually do.

TIM Well, that's up to you, but I think you're crazy!

JANE What's your first lecture on, anyway?

TIM Oh, it's a lecture on the French Revolution.   Q28

JANE The French Revolution! How boring!

TIM It's not boring at all! It was an amazing period of history. It changed everything in Europe. So what's *your* first lecture about?

JANE It's about animal behaviour. It sounds really interesting.

TIM Look, I was on my way to the library. I'm going to get some of these books
out and start reading for the first essay I've got to write.

JANE And what have you got to write about?

TIM Well, you'll never believe it, I think our professor must have a sense of hu-
mour. He's given us the title "Why study history?"   Q29

JANE That's a good one. When you find the answer, let me know!

JIM I'm going to enjoy writing it. Have you been given any writing assignments
yet?

JANE Yes, I've got to write about animal language.   Q30

TIM Hmm! That sounds a challenge. I suppose you'll be off to the zoo to do field
research.

SECTION 4

LECTURER

Welcome to further education Information Week. This is the Physical Education
Faculty's session and I'm the Head of the Faculty. During the course of this morning
we hope to give you a clear idea of what we offer in our training programs and we will
look at the types of courses and the entry requirements, if any, for those courses.
Some of these courses are open to school leavers, but for some you need previous qualifications, or relevant successful employment.

So firstly, the Physical Fitness Instructor's course is offered as a six-month certifi-   *Example*
cate course which includes an important component of personal fitness but there are no
specific entry requirements.

For Sports Administrators we provide a four-month certificate course but you   Q31
should be aware that this is designed for those who are in employment. This employ- Q32
ment must be current and related to sports administration.

For the Sports Psychologist course we offer a one-year diploma course, but this   Q33
diploma course is available only to those who already hold a degree in psychology, so

· 124 ·

you need to make sure you have that before you apply to do this course.

Now...for Physical Education Teachers we offer a four-year degree in education. This degree course is designed for preparing students to teach in primary and secondary schools and <u>needs no prior qualifications</u> as it is entered directly by school leavers.   *Q34*

And lastly <u>for the Recreation Officer's course we offer a six-month certificate</u>. En-   *Q35* try to this course normally includes applicants of a wide range of ages and experiences, but we do not insist on any prerequisites for this course.

Remember that this is a vocational training institute. We train you so that you can take up a particular kind of job. So it is important that you know the main roles of the jobs—what the work is like and what kind of qualities you need to succeed at them.

<u>A Physical Fitness Instructor works in health and fitness centres preparing individ-</u>   *Q36* <u>ual programs for ordinary members of the public</u>. Physical Fitness Instructors prepare routines of exercises to suit the individual client's age and level of fitness.

Sports Administrators run clubs and sporting associations. <u>Their duties include</u>   *Q37* <u>such things as booking playing fields</u> with local councils <u>and organising the schedule of</u> <u>games or events</u> for the club, so they need good organisational skills.

<u>Sports Psychologists spend time with professional athletes helping them</u> approach   *Q38* <u>competition with a positive mental attitude</u> to enable them to achieve their personal best. They do this by improving motivation and concentration or assisting with stress management.

Physical Education or <u>PE Teachers instruct young students in how to exercise,</u>   *Q39* <u>play sport, and do other recreational activities correctly and safely</u>. PE teachers help the development of co-ordination, balance, posture, and flexibility with things like simple catching and throwing skills. They are not expected to be experts in all sports, but must be able to show students the <u>basic techniques involved in a wide range of activ-</u> <u>ities</u>.

Recreation Offcers often find themselves working for local government authorities and local groups. <u>Their aim is to raise people's awareness of healthy lifestyles and im-</u>   *Q40* <u>proved general fitness</u> through arranging recreational activities for groups of all ages from the very young to the elderly.

There are many other job opportunities which our graduates can look forward to. If you are interested in any of these...

SECTION 1

DIANE	Good morning. Diane Davies. Can I help you?
GAVIN	Yes, I'd like to get some insurance for the contents of my home.
DIANE	Fine. When did you move into the house?
GAVIN	<u>A couple of weeks age</u>, and it's an apartment actually. I was told by the *Example*
	landlord that it would be a good idea to get some insurance for the furniture
	and other personal possessions.

Repeat

DIANE	Fine. Well, let's get some details. What kind of apartment is it?	
GAVIN	It's a two-bedroom apartment.	
DIANE	What floor is it on?	
GAVIN	Why do you need to know that?	
DIANE	Because it affects the cost of the insurance. An apartment on the ground	
	floor isn't as protected as others and there's more chance of a break-in.	
GAVIN	Really? I didn't know that. It's on the third, no, ... <u>second floor.</u>	*Q1*
DIANE	Second...and now much is the rent?	
GAVIN	<u>It's $615 per month.</u>	*Q2*
DIANE	Good, and where is it located?	
GAVIN	In Biggins St, South Hills.	
DIANE	I see. And what things did you want to insure?	
GAVIN	Well, what do you recommend?	
DIANE	Well, the most important things are those which you would normally find in	
	a home. Things like the television, fridge and so on.	
GAVIN	I see. Well, I've got a fridge and a stereo system which I've just bought	
	from a friend.	
DIANE	<u>And how much did you pay for the fridge?</u>	*Q3*
GAVIN	Er, $450.	
DIANE	50 OR 15?	
GAVIN	50, <u>and the stereo system cost $1,150.</u>	*Q4*
DIANE	Have you got a television?	
GAVIN	Yes, but it's very old and not worth much.	
DIANE	OK. Well, is there anything else you want to insure?	
GAVIN	Yes, I've got a couple of watches and my CDs and books.	
DIANE	How much do you think they're worth?	

GAVIN	The watches are worth $1,000...
DIANE	For both of them?
GAVIN	No, each one and , all together, <u>the CDs and books cost me about $400.</u>	*Q5*
DIANE	OK, so the value of everything you want to insure is $4,000.
GAVIN	How much will the insurance cost?
DIANE	Let me see, $4,000 divided by...plus 10%...right, so this kind of insurance, er, that's Private Contents insurance, <u>it comes to $184.00 for a</u>	*Q6*
	<u>twelve-month period.</u>
GAVIN	$184.00. Well, that sounds pretty good. OK, I'll take .that policy.

....

GAVIN	Can I arrange the policy over the phone?
DIANE	Sure, just let me get the details down. So that's Mr...
GAVIN	Gavin <u>Murray, that's M-U-R-R-A-Y.</u>	*Q7*
DIANE	And the address is?
GAVIN	It's <u>16C</u> Biggins Street, <u>South Hills.</u>	*Qs 8, 9*
DIANE	OK (*writing*) 16C Biggins Street, South Hills?
GAVIN	That's right, it's two words, 'South Hills'.
DIANE	And your date of birth is?
GAVIN	12 November 1980.
DIANE	And your contact number?
GAVIN	Home phone number is 9872 4855.
DIANE	Right...and er, ...you're Australian?
GAVIN	No... <u>I was born in London,</u> although my mother is from Tasmania.	*Q10*
DIANE	Really? Whereabouts?
GAVIN	Hobart.
DIANE	I see...interesting place. Now, are you working at the moment?
GAVIN	No, I'm a full-time student at Sydney University.
DIANE	Right, good.

SECTION 2

COLLEGE PRESIDENT

Well, good morning, everyone, it's good to see you all here. Welcome to Smith House. Smith House as you may or may not know is one of the oldest residential colleges of the university. As you can see, the building you're in now which contains this main lounge, the dining room, the recreation room, the kitchen and the offices <u>was</u> <u>part of the original old house, built in the 1840s to be used by the family of George</u> *Q11* <u>Smith.</u> That's of course how the house and college got their names. The original house was converted into a residential college for the university in 1940 and since then has continued to be added on to and modernised.

You'll notice when you receive your room allocation in a few minutes that your room number either begins with the letter N, S, or W like this one here, The first Q12 letter refers to the three wings of the college which come away from this main building. Of course the letters represent the three directions—in this case—north, south and west. Each wing has two floors, and so the next number you see is either one, or in this case tow, and this indicates which floor your room is on. The number after that is Q13 your individual room number. So it's quite simple to find any room by going to the Q14 right wing, then floor, and then room number.

....

You'll also notice, when you receive your orientation pack shortly, that there are tow keys. One is the key to your room and only you have that key—and the other is a key to the front door which you've just come through here from the street. This door is closed and locked at 8 pm every night and opened again at 7 am. You'll need your key Q15 if you're coming back to the college between those times. We ask all students to always enter and leave the college through the front door. You will notice at the end of each corridor that there is another door but these are fire doors and are kept locked from the outside. They should only be opened from the inside in case of emergency. Q16

In your fees you've paid a laundry fee which covers the cleaning of bed linen and Q17 towels. All bed linen and towels are clearly embossed with the name Smith House so it's easily identifiable. If you want your other laundry to be done by the college this can be arranged for a small extra ree.

There are only a few rules here at Smith House and we have these rules so that we can all live comfortably together. The most important rule is that there must be no noise after 9 pm. There is also no smoking in the rooms or anywhere inside the college but smoking is permitted on the balconies. Q18

All meals are served in the dining room. Meal times are listed in your orientation pack. Please read these carefully as meal times cannot be changed and if you arrive late Q19 I'm sorry to say you'll just go hungry.

If you're unsure about things, each floor has an elected 'floor senior' who is usually a student in their third or fourth year of study who's been at Smith House for a while. The floor seniors will introduce themselves later today and answer any questions Q20 you have. But for now I'm going to hand you over to Marney who is going to give you the orientation packs and keys. Thanks Marney.

SECTION 3

LYNNE   That essay we have to write...the one on how children learn through the media...how are you planning to write it?

ROBIN	Well, I've given it some thought and I think that the best way to approach it is to divide the essay into two parts. First of all, we'd have to look at some *examples* of each type of media...	
LYNNE	Yes, what they are...then we could describe how we can use each medium so that children can learn something from each one.	
ROBIN	Exactly. Maybe we could draw up a table and look at examples of each medium in turn. Let's see, the different forms of media would be...the print media...	
LYNNE	Here you'd have things like <u>books and newspapers,</u> that sort of thing...	*Q21*
ROBIN	Um, and included in these are the pictorial forms of print media, like maps...	
LYNNE	Yes, <u>maps are really just formal pictures</u>, aren't they? And then there are what we call the audio forms of media...where children can listen. <u>CDs and radios are probably the best examples</u>, because a lot of children have access to these...especially radios.	*Q22* *Q23*
ROBIN	And this would lead into the audio-visual media, which can be seen as well as heard... <u>film, television...and we mustn't forget videos.</u>	*Q24*
LYNNE	Yes, but there's a final category as well... <u>computers, that make up the socalled electronic media.</u> In the United Kingdom and Australia, they say that one in three families has a computer now.	*Q25*
ROBIN	Yes, I believe it. Well that's a good list to start with...we're really getting somewhere with this essay now...so let's move on to when each type of medium could be used. I guess we could start by trying to identify the best situation for each type of media.	
LYNNE	What do you mean?	
ROBIN	I'm talking about whether each medium should be used with different sized groups, For example, we could look at pictures, and ask whether they're more useful for an individual child, a few children together or a full class— in this case, <u>I'd say pictures are best with individual children</u>, because they give them an opportunity to let their imaginations run wild.	*Example*
LYNNE	Yes, I see...	
ROBIN	Let's take tapes next. <u>Although tapes look ideal for individual children, I feel they're best suited to small group work,</u> This way , children don't feel isolated, because they can get help from their friends. <u>Computers are the same...I think they're better with small numbers of children</u> and they're hardly ever useful with a whole class. <u>Videos, however, are ideal for use with everyone present in the class,</u> especially when children have individual activity sheets to help them focus their minds on what's in the video.	*Q26* *Q27* *Q28*

LYNNE   And what about books, what would you recommend for them? <u>Books are</u>   *Q29*
         <u>ideal for children to use by themselves.</u> I know they're used with groups in
         schools, but I wouldn't recommend it. Other pictorial media like <u>maps,</u>
         <u>though, are different</u> ...I'd always plan group work around those...give   *Q30*
         the children a chance to interact and to share ideas.
ROBIN   I agree... teachers often just leave maps on the wall for children to look at
         when they have some free time, but kids really enjoy using them for prob-
         lem solving.
LYNNE   Yes , different people have different ideas I suppose...
ROBIN   Yes, and different teachers recommend different tools for different age
         groups...

SECTION 4

LECTURER

I hope that this first session, which I've called Al Introduction to British Agriculture,
will provide a helpful background to the farm visits you'll be doing next week.

   I think I should start by emphasising that agriculture still accounts for a very important part of this country's economy. We are used to hearing the UK's socitey and e-
conomy described as being 'industrial' or even 'post-industrial', but we mustn't let
this blind us to the fact that agriculture and its supporting industries still account for
around 20% of our Gross National Product.

   This figure is especially impressive, I think, when you bear in mind how very
small a percentage of the UK workforce is employed in agriculture. This is not a recent
development—you would have to go back to 1750 or so to find a majority of the workforce in this country working in agriculture. By the middle of the next century, in
1850 that is, it had fallen sharply to 10%, <u>and then to 3% by the middle of the twen-</u>   *Q31*
<u>tieth century.</u>

   And now just 2% of the workforce contribute 20% of GNP. How is this effi
ciency achieved? Well, my own view is that it owes a great deal to a history, over the
last 50 or 60 years, of intelligent support ty the state, mainly taking the form of helping farmers to plan ahead. Then the two other factors I should mention, both very important, are <u>the high level of training</u> amongst the agricultural workforce. And second-   *Q32*
ly, the recognition by farmers of the <u>value of investing in technology.</u>   *Q33*

   Now, although the UK is a fairly small country, the geology and climate vary a
good deal from region to region. For our purposes today we can divide the country
broadly into three—I've marked them on the map here (*indicates map*).

   The region you'll get to know best, of course, is the north, where we are at present. The land here is generally hilly, · and the soils thin. The climate up here, and

you've already had evidence of this, is generally <u>cool and wet</u>. As you will see next   Q34
week, the typical farm here in the North is a small, family-run concern, producing
mainly <u>wool and timber</u> for the market.   Q35

If we contrast that with the Eastern region, over here (*indicating on map*), the
east is flatter and more low-lying, <u>with fertile soils</u> and a mixed climate. Average farm-   Q36
size is much bigger in the east, and farms are likely to be managed strictly on commercial lines. As for crops, well, the east is the UK's great cereal-producing region.
However, increasingly significant areas are now <u>also given over to high quality vegeta-</u>   Q37
<u>bles</u> for supply direct to the supermarkets.

The third broad region is the west, where it's a different story again. The climate
is <u>warmer than in the north and much wetter</u> than in the east. The resulting rich soils   Q38
in the west provide excellent pasture, and the farms there are quite large, typically
around <u>800 hectares</u>. The main products are milk, cheese and meat.   Q39

So, clearly, there are marked differences between regions, But this does not prevent quite a strong sense of solidarity amongst the farming community as a whole, right
across the country. This solidarity comes in part from the need to present a united front
in dealing with other powerful interest-groups, such as government or the media. It also owes something to the close co-operation between all the agricultural training colleges, through which the great majority of farmers pass at the beginning of their ca-
reers. <u>And a third factor making for solidarity is the national structure of the Farmers'</u>   Q40
<u>Union</u>, of which virtually all farmers are members.

Finally in this short talk, I would like to say a little about the challenges facing
farmers in the next...

TEST 3

SECTION 1

A Excuse me, I'm sorry to bother you, but would you have time to answer a few questions?

B What's it about?

A We're doing some market research for a new television channel starting in two years' time.

B OK, why not?

A Lovely, we'll just work through this form. And if we could start with some personal background information...

B Sure.

A Right, if I could just have your age...

B <u>35</u>.   *Example*

A Right, great...

Repeat

A Right, great. And your job?

B Systems analyst, but for the form I don't know whether it would count as professional or business or what.

A What do you think?

B <u>OK, it's more like business.</u>   *Q1*

A Fine. And would you mind my asking about your salary? Or we can leave it blank.

B No, I don't mind. <u>It's £40,000 a year.</u>   *Q2*

A Thank you. Right...about your current watching habits...what would you say is your main reason for watching TV?

B Well, at work I tend to read for information and what have you, so I'd say that with <u>TV it probably just helps me relax and unwind.</u>   *Q3*

A Fine. And how many hours a day on average do you watch TV?

B Not a lot really...I should say <u>just over an hour.</u>   *Q4*

· ·

A So what are the two main times of the day that you watch TV?

B Well, <u>a little around breakfast time and then it tends to be really late—eleven or   *Q5*
   even midnight</u>—when I've finished work.

A And what sort of programmes do you go for?

B Some news bulletins but I also really like to put my feet up with some of the old comedy shows.

A Fine. And turning to the new channel...which type of programmes would you like to see more of?

B Well, I certainly don't think we need any more factual programmes like news and documentaries. I think we need more about things like local information...you *Q6* know, providing a service for the community. And in the same vein, perhaps more for younger viewers...you know, good quality stuff. *Q6*

A Ah ha. And if you had to give the new directors some specific advice when they set up the channel, what advice would you give them?

B I think I'd advise them to pay a lot of attention to the quality of the actual broad- *Q7* cast, you know, the sound system. People are very fussy these days about that and in general I think they ought to do lots more of these kinds of interview, you *Q7* know, talking with their potential customers.

A Oh, I'm glad you think it's valuable!

B Certainly...yeah.

A Good. OK, this will be a commercial channel of course, but how often do you think it is tolerable to have adverts?

B Well out of that list I'd say every quarter of an hour. I don't think we can complain *Q8* about that, as long as they don't last for ten minutes each time!

A Quite. And ...would you be willing to attend any of our special promotions for the new channel?

B Yes, I'd be very happy to, as long as they're held here in my area. *Q9*

A OK, I'll make a note of that. And finally, may we put you on our mailing list?

B Well, I'd prefer not... except for the information about the promotion you men- *Q10* tioned.

A Can I have your name and address?

B Of course...here's my card.

A Oh, lovely...and thank you very much for your time and we look forward to see-ing you.

B Yes, indeed. Um, thanks.

SECTION 2

ELIZABETH   OK, well, good morning everybody! My name's Elizabeth Reed and I'm your Assistant Welfare Officer. What I'd like to do now is tell you a little more about some of the er...the social facilities available on the campus, and also to tell you something about what the town has to offer.

As you probably know already, the Student Union Building is the main centre of social life here, as indeed it is in most British

Universities. The Union runs a weekly programme of events for all tastes...oh everything from discos to talks by guest speakers. <u>Many of these events are fund raising activities for charities,</u> which the Union takes very seriously. They manage <u>the Students' Union paper-shop, selling magazines and newspapers,</u> as well as stationery, sweets and so on. Um...Then...er, let me see...there's <u>the Ticket Shop, where you can get some very good deals on,</u> well for example, <u>coaches to London or inexpensive charter flights,</u> as cheap as <u>you'll get anywhere</u> people say, or tickets for big pop groups playing here or at other venues all over the country, or plays in London—oh and we mustn't forget <u>the Union Cafeteria and the Big New Diner</u>...Er...yes? Did you have a question?

STUDENT   Yes, does the Union also provide help with any problems, I mean advice on financial problems, for example? Or does the University provide that?

ELIZABETH   Yes, the Union run their own advice service, <u>offering help with financial matters such as grants.</u> I am sure you realise anything *medical* should be discussed with the University Medical Service, which also has an excellent counselling centre. I think that was made clear yesterday. However <u>the Union has its own officer who can give advice on legal problems.</u>

Now, onto Radford. For a town of its size, Radford has some unusually good leisure and community facilities and has quite a good shopping centre, with an interesting range of shops. As you go into Radford, there's a new...well, quite new... <u>Olympic-size swimming pool. That's on the outskirts</u> at a place called Renton. <u>Above the pool there's a hi-tech fitness centre.</u> Are there any ice skaters here? No? Oh, pity! The facilities for ice-skating are excellent. Well, <u>the new Metro Tower, right in the centre of town has got an ice rink</u> and a sports hall for squash, badminton, volleyball and several other indoor sports. <u>And in the same building there's a new cinema</u> with six screens. Er...then, let me see, <u>in the main square, just two minutes' walk from the Metro Tower,</u> there's the Theatre Royal, which often gets London productions on tour...and in the streets nearby you can find a good range of inexpensive restaurants including Indian, Chinese, Thai and...

Q11
Q12
Q13
Q14

Q15

Q16

Example
Q17
Q18
Q19
Q20

SECTION 3

DR SIMON	OK, welcome back to the new term. Hope you've had a good break and that you're looking forward to writing your dissertation...What I'd like to do in this session is give you the opportunity to ask questions on writing the dissertation...requirements, milestones...who to see when you need help. It's very informal...it may all be written on paper, but it's nice to get it confirmed. So anything you'd like to ask?	
ANDY	Dr Simon, is there a fixed hand-in date yet?	
DR SIMON	Right. I <u>can confirm that that's 21 May,</u> not 20 as we first stated. OK? ...Jane?	*Q21*
JANE	What about the word limit?	
DR SIMON	Well we try to be pretty flexible on this, but in broad terms it's <u>18 – 20,000.</u>	*Q22*
JANE	Ah...	
DR SIMON	And you can choose your topics ... anything from Years 2 and 3 ... Yes?	
JANE	I still haven't got any idea what I want to do it on. Who...?	
DR SIMON	Well, you should see your course tutor to agree on your final title and you should also be aware that <u>there's a special programme running on research methods</u> for anyone who wants some extra help on that.	*Q23*
JANE	Can I just check on the deadlines for everything?	
DR SIMON	Yes, sure. Look, let me write it on the board...when the different stages have to be completed. First of all you've got to work on your basic bibliography, and that's due in to your course tutor by 31 January...which is just two weeks away, so you'd better get a move on on that.	
ANDY	Do we have to have our own draft plan by then?	
DR SIMON	No, <u>your draft plan is due on 7 February,</u> which is a week later, so that should give you plenty of time.	*Q24*
JANE	And <u>when do we have to be doing the research?</u>	*Q25*
DR SIMON	That's over a one-month period...essentially February to March.	
ANDY	And the write up?	
DR SIMON	Well, <u>you can't really get going on your writing until you've got quite a bit of the research done, so that's really March to May,</u> with the hand in date on 21st. Any more questions?	*Q26*

ANDY	Well, sir, just some advice really. It's about computers...would you advise us to buy one?
DR SIMON	What can I say, Andy? I know it's a massive expense, but <u>I really feel that it will be of great benefit</u>...you can always look in the Student Union adverts for second hand ones. Yes?
JANE	I've been looking at some of last year's dissertations.
ANDY	Is that a good idea, sir? I heard...
DR SIMON	Well, I don't think you should read them in detail too early or you might end up taking more of their ideas than you realise. <u>But yes...it really is the best guide you can have</u> to the expectations of the...of what's expected when you write a dissertation.
ANDY	Sorry, Jane, I interrupted you.
JANE	That's OK. It's just that they did a lot of research using questionnaires...is that a good idea?
DR SIMON	I think questionnaires are very good at telling you how people fill in questionnaires, but <u>to be frank they tell you very little else</u>. Avoid them!
ANDY	About interviews...is it OK if we interview you?
DR SIMON	<u>The tutors? I don't see why not;</u> they don't have any special contribution to make, but <u>you can if you want.</u> There's a whole section on this issue in the Research Guide. I'm afraid it's slightly out of date, and you're probably better talking to the tutor on the Research Methods course, but you might find it useful to start there.
ANDY/JANE	OK, thanks.
DR SIMON	OK...well, great, I hope that sorted a few things out. You can always come and see me or drop me a note if you've got any more queries.
ANDY/JANE	Fine.
DR SIMON	OK, Thanks...

The Q markers appear to the right: *Q27*, *Q28*, *Q29*, *Q30*.

SECTION 4

LECTURER

Good morning. This morning we are continuing our look at Australia and its natural problems. Actually dryness, or aridity, as it is generally called by geographers, is probably the most challenging of Australia's natural problems and so it is very important in this course for you to have a good understanding of the subject. For Australia, water is a precious resource and its wise management is of the greatest importance.

As I have said, Australia is a dry continent, <u>second only to Antarctica</u> in its lack *Q31* of rainfall. Long hours of hot sunshine and searing winds give Australia an extremely high rate of evaporation, far more than in most other countries. It is estimated that approximately <u>87% of Australia's rainfall is lost through evaporation, compared with just</u> <u>over 60% in Europe and Africa</u> and 48% in North America. You generally think of Africa as being a very hot and dry place, but it is not in comparison with Australia. In many parts of Australia standing water, that is dams, puddles and so forth, dry up rapidly and some rainfall barely penetrates the soil. The reason for this is that <u>the moisture is absorbed by thirsty plants.</u>

Some parts of Australia are dry because <u>rainwater seeps quickly through sandy soils and into the rock below.</u> In parts of Australia this water which seeps through the sandy soil collects underground to form underground lakes. Water from these subterranean lakes can be pumped to the surface and tapped and so used for various purposes above the ground. In fact, extensive underground water resources are available over more than half of Australia's land area, but most of the water is too salty to be used for human consumption or for the irrigation of crops. However, <u>most inland farmers do rely on this water for watering their animals</u> and, where possible, to a lesser extent for irrigation.

Underground water can flow very large distances and can be kept in underground reservoirs for a very long time. Water from these underground reservoirs bubbles to the surface as springs in some parts of the country, and <u>these fare sources of permanent water</u> were vital to early explorers of inland Australia, and to other pioneers last century, who used the springs for survival. But in many places levels have fallen drastically through continuous use over the years. This has necessitated the pumping of the water to the surface. Remarkably, <u>underground water sources in Australia supply about 18% of total water consumption.</u> So you can see it is quite an important source of water in this dry land.

So most of the consumption of water in Australia comes from water which is kept above ground. More than 300 dams regulate river flows around the country. The dams store water for a variety of functions, <u>the rural irrigation of crops</u>, without which many productive areas of the country would not be able to be farmed; <u>the regulation of flooding,</u> a serious problem which will be dealt with later in the course; and last but not least, the harnessing of the force of gravity for <u>the generation of electricity.</u>

That is all we have time for this morning, but you will be able to do further study on this important area in the library. I have a handout here with references on the subject, so if you are interested, please come up to the desk and take a copy.

Next week's lecture is a case study of an outback farm and...

SECTION 1

AGENT	Good morning. MIC House Agency.
PAUL	Good morning. I'm ringing about the problems I've been having with my a-partment.
AGENT	Yes, of course. If I can just take a few details first...What's your name?
PAUL	Paul Smiley.
AGENT	How do you spell that?
PAUL	S-M-I-L-E-Y.

Example

Repeat

AGENT	OK, and what's the address?	
PAUL	Apartment 2, <u>16 Rose Lane.</u>	*Q1*
AGENT	Rose Lane...and that's in...?	
PAUL	In Newton.	
AGENT	Oh yes, I know the property. Could I just ask how long is the lease?	
PAUL	It's for one year.	
AGENT	And you moved in...?	
PAUL	Last week, <u>on 27th June.</u>	*Q2*
AGENT	Fine, thank you.	

AGENT	And what are the problems that you've been having?	
PAUL	Well, no one thing is really dangerous or anything, but you know, it's just been building up.	
AGENT	Yes, of course.	
PAUL	Well the first thing is the washing machine. It's been leaking a little and it's beginning to get worse. Because we have a small child, <u>we really need to get that done straight away.</u>	*Example*
AGENT	OK...that's a washing machine for immediate repair.	
PAUL	And then there's a niggling problem with the cooker...	
AGENT	Ah ha...	
PAUL	<u>The door's broken.</u>	*Q3*
AGENT	Right.	
PAUL	It's nothing serious and it can be used, but <u>if you can send someone over in the next couple of weeks or so</u> that'd be great.	*Q4*
AGENT	Fine, I've got that.	

PAUL	Then we are worried about all the windows.
AGENT	Are they broken?
PAUL	No, but <u>there are no locks on them</u>...and you know with the insurance *Q5* these days...
AGENT	And when would you like those done?
PAUL	Oh, that's not really urgent...but you never know when there's going to be a break-in...
AGENT	No, we'll get those done for you next week, don't worry.
PAUL	And then <u>there's the bathroom light...it's getting quite annoying. It flick-</u> *Q6* <u>ers quite badly</u> and it's giving me headaches. <u>I'd really like to get that re-</u> *Q7* <u>placed right away.</u>
AGENT	That's no problem.
PAUL	And then the last thing on the list <u>is the kitchen curtains. They're torn.</u> *Q8*
AGENT	Oh, right. We do have quite a few spare ones in stock and <u>can get those to</u> *Q9* <u>you in the next week,</u> if that's alright with you?
PAUL	Yes, that'd be fine.
AGENT	Anything else?
PAUL	No, that's all.
AGENT	OK, fine. What we'll do is get someone over to you this afternoon, if you're in.
PAUL	Well, I'm going to be out for a short time.
AGENT	Well you tell us your preferred times.
PAUL	Well <u>the best time is about 1.00.</u> *Q10*
AGENT	I'll have to check that with him. And if he can't make it then, what would be your second preference?
PAUL	<u>Any time up to 5 pm would be fine.</u> *Q10*
AGENT	OK, I've made a note of that.
PAUL	Great, well thanks very much for your help.
AGENT	That's fine. Thank you for calling.
PAUL	Goodbye.
AGENT	Goodbye.

SECTION 2

RECREATION OFFICER

Great. Well, hi, everyone! My name's Jody and I'm one of the four recreation offi-
cers here at Rainforest Lodge. My job is to make sure that you all have a great stay here
with us and go away feeling relaxed and refreshed. As you can see, we're literally in
the middle of nowhere at the Lodge. <u>There are no newspapers or TVs</u> and there's only *Q11*

one phone and that's in the office. The Lodge is a complete 'getaway from it all' experience: a place to unwind and appreciate the world without a lot of interruptions and distractions.

From your cabin balcony you'll find that you can't see anyone else and the only noise you should hear is the birds. When the luggage comes, one of the guys will take it across to your cabin for you and make sure you know the way back here to the main centre for dinner in the restaurant. <u>Dinner will be served in about an hour or so.</u>   Q12

All the times of each day's activities are printed on the blue sheet you should have got in the information guides that were handed out on the coach. Each Explorer trip has a different focus, so it doesn't matter how many you do or on what day, because there's always something new to discover in the rainforest.

Tomorrow I think we've still got places on the Orchid and Fungi Tour. This is on foot and takes you to different parts of the rainforest. Or, if you'd prefer, there's the <u>Four-Wheel-Drive tour to the waterfalls</u>, or the fishing trip where I promise you we'll   Q13
catch some lunch, and last but not least, the famous <u>Crocodile Cruise that leaves at 11</u>   Q14
<u>am</u> each day. (Just in time for the crocodile's lunch!) Plenty to choose from here at Rainforest Lodge or just sit on your balcony, relax and unwind and enjoy the views. In the evenings there is the Spotlight Tour, one of my favourites. <u>The Spotlight Tour</u>   Q15
<u>leaves at sundown</u> and lets you catch a glimpse of some more of the rainforest's wildlife as it comes out at dusk to feed. That's a great trip and if you can, I'd really try to make sure you do it during your stay.

You've chosen to visit the rainforest in March, which is just at the end of the wet season, so you'll soon notice how well the waterfalls are running and also how damp the ground is. Things can tend to get a bit slippery, too, so <u>if you didn't bring any walk-</u>   Q16
<u>ing boots I'd advise you to hire some</u> from the office. <u>You'll also be much better off in</u>   Q17
<u>long trousers</u> rather than shorts because they will give your legs more protection, <u>and</u>
<u>socks are a good idea too.</u>   Q18

There's no need to be nervous of the rainforest provided that you treat it with respect and common sense. Most of the animals and wildlife are gentle and harmless. <u>There are some venomous snakes to beware of</u>, but really they're much more frightened   Q19
of you than you are of them. The other thing is that <u>certain plants can cause irritation</u> if   Q20
you touch them with bare skin.

Well, that's about all for the time being. The guys are here to take you and your luggage to the cabins...

SECTION 3

COUNSELLOR   Hello, John, What can I do for you?

JOHN	Well, I heard about these counselling sessions from a friend doing a science course and I was really interested. I think they should be compulsory really.	
COUNSELLOR	Well to be quite honest, John, I think they *would* be useful for everybody but well, everybody has their own way of going about things. <u>I prefer people just to drop in when they can.</u>	*Q21*
JOHN	Yes.	
COUNSELLOR	I find that talking to students about the requirements of a course helps to clarify what needs to be done. I mean the biggest difference between college and school is that <u>new college students really have to do a lot of work on their own</u>, and it's sometimes useful to get advice on how to take control of your time and work effectively.	*Q22*
JOHN	Yes. I mean, it seems like a very light workload until assignment time comes and then I seem to be working all night sometimes. I'm not the only one. It's ridiculous. The resource centre is very good <u>but it closes so early</u>. It's in the library and so you'd think you could use it more. It's a real problem for me.	*Q23*
COUNSELLOR	Well, you're certainly not the only person in that position, as I'm sure you've found. It really comes down to using every available hour in a systematic way. If you do this with a plan, then <u>you'll find that you still have time for yourself and your hobbies as well.</u>	*Q24*
JOHN	Yeah. I've heard from Thomas that you made him a sort of plan like this, and he's going away for the weekend with all his work handed in, whereas I haven't even started.	
COUNSELLOR	<u>I need to find out a few more things about you first.</u> I'll give you this form to fill in about your lectures and things before you leave.	*Q25*

COUNSELLOR	Now, what are your main problems?	
JOHN	Well, what most concerns me is I'm still not doing very well in my assignments.	
COUNSELLOR	Well, I know that you plan your writing carefully, but this can come to nothing if the assignment doesn't answer the question. That really is the key. You must read the question carefully and give it a great deal of thought before you even start planning or writing your first draft. <u>It's also vital to check your work for errors.</u> Everybody makes them, and they can influence the person marking the work. So, <u>always take time at the end to check what you have written.</u>	*Q26* *Q26*

JOHN	As far as listening is concerned, I find it hard to keep up sometimes in lectures, especially two-hour ones. I sometimes just seem to go off into a dream.	
COUNSELLOR	It's a good idea to find out from your lecturers <u>if they mind you recording the lectures.</u> You only need one of those small cassette recorders. The quality is pretty good and a second listening can really clarify things. Something else you can do is <u>check your notes with a friend</u> after the lecture.	*Q27* *Q28*
JOHN	Yes. That's a good idea. Thanks. It's hard to do all that all the time though, especially when there's so much reading to do.	
COUNSELLOR	Yes. It's important, though, not to confine yourself to reading on your subject. <u>You should also read things of general interest</u> that appeal to you. You know, novels, newspapers, that kind of thing. <u>Do you have a good dictionary?</u>	*Q29* *Q30*
JOHN	Not really. I've never bothered with one.	
COUNSELLOR	Mmmm. <u>It would probably be a good idea to get one.</u> Dictionaries are not expensive and they can help a lot. Also you can underline or highlight new words and...	*Q30*

SECTION 4

TUTOR	Well, good afternoon. In today's session John Upton will be sharing some of the findings of his research project from last term. John...	
JOHN	Thanks. Well, first of all, a little bit about the background to the project. Our title, as you can see, is pretty straightforward: 'car safety'. But these days there's a lot more to it than the usual injunctions about drinking and driving or speeding. <u>I had been interested and horrified by several newspaper reports</u> on what people call 'road rage'. For example the famous incident of a man getting out of his car in a car park and hitting the driver of a van who had overtaken him earlier. It seemed to me that there were almost as many serious problems when cars were parked...i.e. were stationary...as when they were travelling at 90 miles an hour. So I decided to make this the focus of the project.	*Q31*
	<u>For our research we depended mainly on talking to individuals, asking them questions rather than using written questionnaires.</u> We stopped people at a selected garage on the motorway over a two-day period, and asked them questions about what they'd observed or experienced themselves. Our respondents were both men and women, <u>but the women were just slightly in the majority.</u> We were pleased by the public's willingness to stop and	*Q32* *Q33*

chat to us...in the end <u>we talked to a total of 135 drivers</u> over those two   *Q34*
days.

So what were our findings? Well, as you can see, 93% of respondents had had some kind of problem. A surprisingly large percentage—24% had had their car damaged in some way, but <u>the main type of inci-   *Q35*
dent was being shouted at</u> — 79% had experienced that. 15% had experienced violence on their own persons...they'd actually been hit by someone. The police tended only to be informed when there was physical violence involved.

So what strategies had people developed to ensure their own safety? Let's have a look at the figures here. Well, first of all, it was quite striking that there were often distinct answers from the men and women. <u>It   *Example*
was mainly women, for example, who said one shouldn't ever stop to find   *Q36*
out how to get somewhere.</u> Whereas <u>it was men who said you should try to
avoid looking directly at other drivers.</u> Both men and ...oh sorry no... <u>it   *Q37*
was women who said you had to tell someone when you were due to get to a
particular destination.</u> Then, I had thought that it would be mainly men,
but <u>both sexes made the point that it's much safer to get keys out well in   *Q38*
advance as</u> you go towards your car. <u>Men</u> were very aware that muggers or
whatever might be concealed behind the car. They <u>also made the point that   *Q39*
you should leave plenty of room when you park your car</u> so you can make a
quick getaway if you need to. Finally, <u>locking doors at all times</u>...men   *Q40*
didn't think it was quite as important as women, <u>but both gave it a high</u>
<u>safety rating.</u>

When we asked them what they thought the best improvements had
been in the last five years in helping with road rage problems...

Answer Keys

TEST 1

LISTENING

Each question correctly answered scores 1 mark. **CORRECT SPELLING NEEDED IN ALL AN-SWERS.** (*Where alternative spellings are accepted, these are stated in the Key.*)

Section 1, Questions 1 − 10

1. Black
2. 2085
3. 9456 1309
4. 2020BD
5. July
6. B ⎫
7. D ⎬ *in any order*
8. F ⎭
9. $25/twenty-five dollars (refundable)
10. next week//in a week//in one week//the following week

Section 2, Questions 11 − 20

11. route book
12. 900/nine hundred miles **NOT** 900
13. North/N Africa **NOT** Africa
14. A
15. C
16. B ⎫
17. C ⎬ *in any order*
18. E ⎭
19. B ⎫
20. D ⎬ *in either order*

Section 3, Questions 21 − 30

21. (on) Friday
22. Biology
23. 57/fifty-seven (books)
24. 43/forty-three (books)
25. Wed/Wednesday **NOT** the day after
26. (she) record(s) them/lectures//she use(s) a (tape/cassette) recorder/recording
27. skimming// (he) skims (books) / (a book) //skim (the) book first//skim reading
28. (The) French Revolution
29. Why study history (?)
30. animal language// (the) language of animals **NOT** language

Section 4, Questions 31 − 40

31. 4/four-month certificate/cert (course)
32. (current) employment//job
33. 1/one-year diploma **ACCEPT** dyploma
34. none//no (prior) qualifications/quals
35. 6/six-month certificate/cert (course)
36. C   37. F   38. B
39. G   40. D

If you score...

0 − 18	19 − 25	26 − 40
you are highly unlikely to get and acceptable score under examination conditions and we recommend that you spend a lot of time improving your English before you take IELTS	you may get an acceptable score under examination conditions but we recommend that you think about having more practice or lessons before you take IELTS	you are likely to get an acceptable score under examination conditions but remember that different institutions will find different scores acceptable

ACADEMIC READING

Each question correctly answered scores 1 mark.

Reading Passage 1 , Questions 1 – 13

1. A
2. A
3. B
4. C
5. B
6. runways and taxiways
7. terminal building site
8. sand
9. stiff clay
10. Lantau Island ⎫
11. sea walls ⎬ *in either order*
12. rainfall
13. geotextile

Reading Passage 2 , Questions 14 – 27

14. viii
15. ii
16. iv
17. ix
18. vii
19. 1946
20. (the) wealthy (members) (of) (society)
21. social, economic, environmental
22. (the) 1970s
23. NOT GIVEN
24. YES
25. NO
26. NO
27. NOT GIVEN

Reading Passage 3 , Questions 28 – 40

28. CH
29. MC
30. MC
31. SH
32. SH
33. MC
34. HTK
35. SH
36. NOT GIVEN
37. YES
38. YES
39. YES
40. NO

If you score...

0 – 13	14 – 22	23 – 40
you are highly unlikely to get an acceptable score under examination conditions and we recommend that you spend a lot of time improving your English before you take IELTS	you may get an acceptable score under examination conditions but we recommend that you think about having more practice or lessons before you take IELTS	you are likely to get an acceptable score under examination conditions but remember that different institutions will find different scores acceptable

LISTENING

Each question correctly answered scores 1 mark. **CORRECT SPELLING NEEDED IN ALL AN-SWERS.** (*Where alternative spellings are accepted, these are stated in the Key.*)

Section 1, Questions 1 − 10

1. B
2. A
3. fridge/refrigerator
4. stereo (system)
5. books
6. ($ dollars) 184 **NOT** per month/monthly
7. Murray
8. 16C
9. South Hills
10. English//British

Section 2, Questions 11 − 20

11. B
12. north//N
13. (2nd/second) floor (number)
14. room (number)
15. 8 pm (and 7 am)
16. (the) fire/emergency doors
17. laundry//washing
18. (the) balconies **ACCEPT** balconys
19. meal times
20. (elected) floor senior(s)

Section 3, Questions 21 − 30

21. newspaper(s)
22. map(s)
23. radio(s)
24. television//TV
25. computer(s)
26. B
27. B
28. C
29. A
30. B

Section 4, Questions 31 − 40

31. A
32. training
33. technology **ACCEPT** tecknology/teknology
34. cool (and) wet (*both for one mark*)
35. wool (and) timber (*both for one mark*)
36. fertile soil(s) /land/earth/ground
37. (high quality) vegetables/vegs
38. warm (and) wet (*both for one mark*)
39. 800 // eight hundred
40. B

If you score...

0 − 16	17 − 25	26 − 40
you are highly unlikely to get an acceptable score under examination conditions and we recommend that you spend a lot of time improving your English before you take IELTS	you may get an acceptable score under examination conditions but we recommend that you think about having more practice or lessons before you take IELTS	you are likely to get an acceptable score under examination conditions but remember that different institutions will find different scores acceptable

ACADEMIC READING

Each question correctly answered scores 1 mark.

Reading Passage 1 , Questions 1 – 13

1. C
2. A
3. C
4. B
5. B
6. benchmarking
7. (a range of) service delivery
8. (performance) measures
9. productivity
10. (') Take Charge (')
11. feedback
12. employee(s') //staff
13. 30 days

Reading Passage 2 , Questions 14 – 26

14. major consequences
15. surveys
16. sales literature
17. Eastern Europe//Far East//Russia//Arab world //Latin America //French-speaking Africa
18. C
19. B

20. C
21. (industrial) training (schemes) ⎫
22. translation services   ⎬ *in any*
23. (part-time) language courses   ⎭ *order*
24. (technical) glossaries
25. D
26. A

Reading Passage 3 , Questions 27 – 40

27. ii
28. i
29. v
30. vi
31. D
32. C
33. F
34. G
35. NO
36. YES
37. NO
38. YES
39. NOT GIVEN
40. YES

If you score...

0 – 14	15 – 22	23 – 40
you are highly unlikely to get an acceptable score under examination conditions and we recommend that you spend a lot of time improving your English before you take IELTS	you may get an acceptable score under examination conditions but we recommend that you think about having more practice or lessons before you take IELTS	you are likely to get an acceptable score under examination conditions but remember that different institutions will find different scores acceptable

LISTENING

Each question correctly answered scores 1 mark. **CORRECT SPELLING NEEDED IN ALL AN-SWERS.** (*Where alternative spellings are accepted, these are stated in the Key.*)

Section 1, Questions 1 - 10

1. B
2. C
3. A
4. B
5. *both required for one mark, either order*
AE
6. *both required for one mark, either order*
AC
7. *both required for one mark, either order*
CE
8. B
9. C
10. B

Section 2, Questions 11 - 20

11. A ⎫
12. C ⎪ *in any order*
13. E ⎬
14. G ⎭
15. B ⎫ *in either order*
16. E ⎭
17. C
18. A
19. A
20. B

Section 3, Questions 21 - 30

21. 21 May *or acceptable alternatives*
22. 18,000 - 20,000 // 18 - 20,000 *must have both numbers* (or in words)
23. research methods **NOT** research
24. (draft) plan
25. (do/carry out/conduct) research
26. March (to) May (*both for one mark*)
27. A
28. A
29. C
30. B

Section 4, Questions 31 - 40

31. C
32. B
33. C
34. B
35. B
36. C
37. A
38. B ⎫
39. D ⎬ *in any order*
40. E ⎭

If you score...

0 - 17	18 - 25	26 - 40
you are highly unlikely to get an acceptable score under examination conditions and we recommend that you spend a lot of time improving your English before you take IELTS	you may get an acceptable score under examination conditions but we recommend that you think about having more practice or lessons before you take IELTS	you are likely to get an acceptable score under examination conditions but remember that different institutions will find different scores acceptable

ACADEMIC READING

Each question correctly answered scores 1 mark.

Reading Passage 1, Questions 1 – 13

1. NO
2. NO
3. NO
4. YES
5. NOT GIVEN
6. NO
7. YES
8. (local) businesses
9. (work/working) schedule//rostering//roster(s)
10. excessive
11. voluntary absence/absenteeism
12. twenty//20
13. communication

Reading Passage 2, Questions 14 – 26

14. C
15. F
16. E
17. H
18. A
19. D
20. NOT GIVEN
21. NO
22. NOT GIVEN
23. YES
24. YES
25. YES
26. NO

Reading Passage 3, Questions 27 – 40

27. iv
28. vii
29. viii
30. iii
31. ii
32. i
33. X
34. B
35. B
36. E
37. A
38. B
39. D
40. E

If you score...

0 – 15	16 – 24	25 – 40
you are highly unlikely to get an acceptable score under examination conditions and we recommend that you spend a lot of time improving your English before you take IELTS	you may get an acceptable score under examination conditions but we recommend that you think about having more practice or lessons before you take IELTS	you are likely to get an acceptable score under examination conditions but remember that different institutions will find different scores acceptable

TEST 4

LISTENING

Each question correctly answered scores 1 mark. **CORRECT SPELLING NEEDED IN ALL ANSWERS.** *(Where alternative spellings are accepted, these are stated in the Key.)*

Section 1, Questions 1 – 10

1. 16 Rose Lane
2. 27 (th) June *or acceptable alternatives*
3. door broken//broken door
4. C
5. no locks (on them) //need locks
6. bathroom light
7. A
8. kitchen curtains
9. B
10. 1 (pm) (and) 5 (pm)

Section 2, Questions 11 – 20

11. B
12. C
13. waterfall(s)//water fall(s)//water-fall(s)
14. eleven/11.00//11 (am)
15. Spotlight (tour)
16. walking boots ⎫
17. socks   ⎬ *in any order*
18. long trousers ⎭
19. (venomous/poisonous) snakes ⎫ *in either*
20. (certain) plants   ⎬ *order*

Section 3, Questions 21 – 30

21. B
22. B
23. A
24. C
25. C
26. check (over) (your) work/errors//revise (work)
27. record
28. (a) friend **ACCEPT** friend
29. general interest **NOT** interest
30. dictionary

Section 4, Questions 31 – 40

31. B
32. A
33. A
34. B
35. C
36. B
37. A
38. C
39. B
40. C

If you score...

0 – 18	19 – 26	27 – 40
you are highly unlikely to get an acceptable score under examination conditions and we recommend that you spend a lot of time improving your English before you take IELTS	you may get an acceptable score under examination conditions but we recommend that you think about having more practice or lessons before you take IELTS	you are likely to get an acceptable score under examination conditions but remember that different institutions will find different scores acceptable

ACADEMIC READING

Each question correctly answered scores 1 mark.

Reading Passage 1 , Questions 1 – 13

1. YES
2. NO
3. YES
4. NOT GIVEN
5. NO
6. NOT GIVEN
7. B
8. B
9. C
10. honesty and openness
11. consumers
12. armchair ethicals
13. social record

Reading Passage 2 ; Questions 14 – 26

14. D
15. B
16. D
17. C
18. NO
19. YES
20. YES
21. NOT GIVEN
22. F
23. C
24. J
25. I
26. C

Reading Passage 3 , Questions 27 – 40

27. Apollo (space) programme
28. (early) next century
29. 7,000
30. disease
31. muscular dystrophy
32. cystic fibrosis
33. D
34. C
35. B
36. C
37. D
38. B
39. A
40. A

If you score...

0 – 14	15 – 23	24 – 40
you are highly unlikely to get an acceptable score under examination conditions and we recommend that you spend a lot of time improving your English before you take IELTS	you may get an acceptable score under examination conditions but we recommend that you think about having more practice or lessons before you take IELTS	you are likely to get an acceptable score under examination conditions but remember that different institutions will find different scores acceptable

GENERAL TRAINING TEST A

READING

Section 1, Questions 1 – 13

1. FALSE
2. TRUE
3. TRUE
4. NOT GIVEN
5. FALSE
6. D ⎫
7. I ⎭ *in either order*
8. G ⎫
9. J ⎭ *in either order*
10. B ⎫
11. C ⎭ *in either order*
12. E ⎫
13. K ⎭ *in either order*

Section 2, Questions 14 – 26

14. NOT GIVEN
15. TRUE
16. TRUE
17. FALSE
18. NOT GIVEN
19. TRUE
20. TRUE
21. vi
22. viii
23. x
24. ii
25. v
26. vii

Section 3, Questions 27 – 40

27. 1772
28. 1781
29. 1787
30. 1977
31. 1986
32. YES
33. NO
34. NOT GIVEN
35. YES
36. NOT GIVEN
37. georgium.sidus
38. Herschel
39. James L. Elliot
40. Miranda

If you score...

0 – 19	20 – 27	28 – 40
you are highly unlikely to get an acceptable score under examination conditions and we recommend that you spend a lot of time improving your English before you take IELTS	you may get an acceptable score under examination conditions but we recommend that you think about having more practice or lessons before you take IELTS	you are likely to get an acceptable score under examination conditions but remember that different institutions will find different scores acceptable

· 152 ·

GENERAL TRAINING TEST B

READING

Section 1 , Questions 1 – 13

1. C
2. B
3. B
4. A
5. A
6. A
7. C
8. FALSE
9. TRUE
10. NOT GIVEN
11. FALSE
12. FALSE
13. NOT GIVEN

Section 2 , Questions 14 – 26

14. TRUE
15. FALSE
16. NOT GIVEN
17. FALSE
18. TRUE
19. NOT GIVEN
20. TRUE

21. iv
22. vi
23. vii
24. ix
25. iii
26. i

Section 3 , Questions 27 – 40

27. v
28. vii
29. iv
30. i
31. viii
32. iii
33. transmitted (**NOT** sent) (electronically)
34. (photographic) film/negative(s)
35. (aluminium) printing plates
36. programmed
37. (tough) wrapping//damaged paper
38. weighed
39. paster robot(s)
40. storage area

If you score...

0 – 18	19 – 26	27 – 40
you are highly unlikely to get an acceptable score under examination conditions and we recommend that you spend a lot of time improving your English before you take IELTS	you may get an acceptable score under examination conditions but we recommend that you think about having more practice or lessons before you take IELTS	you are likely to get an acceptable score under examination conditions but remember that different institutions will find different scores acceptable

Model and Sample Answers for Writing Tasks

TEST 1, WRITING TASK 1

MODEL ANSWER

This model has been prepared by an examiner as an example of a very good answer. However, please note that this is just one example out of many possible approaches.

The chart shows that the percentage of British households with a range of consumer durables steadily increased between 1972 and 1983. The greatest increase was in telephone ownership, rising from 42% in 1972 to 77% in 1983. Next came central heating ownership, rising from 37% of households in 1972 to 64% in 1983. The percentage of households with a refrigerator rose 21% over the same period and of those with a washing machine by 14%. Households with vacuum-cleaners, televisions and dishwashers increased by 8%, 5% and 2% respectively. In 1983, the year of their introduction, 18% of households had a video recorder.

The significant social changes reflected in the statistics are that over the period the proportion of British houses with central heating rose from one to two thirds, and of those with a phone from under a half to over three-quarters. Together with the big increases in the ownership of washing machines and refrigerators, they are evidence of both rising living standards and the trend to lifestyles based on comfort and convenience.

TEST 1, WRITING TASK 2

MODEL ANSWER

This model has been prepared by an examiner as an example of a very good answer. However, please note that this is just one example out of many possible approaches.

I believe that child-rearing should be the responsibility of both parents and that, whilst the roles within that partnership may be different, they are nevertheless equal in importance. In some societies, it has been made easier over the years for single parents to raise children on their own. However, this does not mean that the traditional family, with both parents providing emotional support and role-models for their children, is not the most satisfactory way of bringing up children.

Of crucial importance, in my opinion, is how we define 'responsible for bringing the children up'. At its simplest, it could mean giving the financial support necessary to provide a home, food and clothes and making sure the child is safe and receives an adequate education. This would be the basic definition.

There is, however, another possible way of defining that part of the quotation. That would say it is not just the father's responsibility to provide the basics for his children, while his wife involves herself in the everyday activity of bringing them up. Rather, he should share those daily duties, spend as much time as his job allows with his children, play with them, read to them, help directly with their education, participate very fully in their lives and encourage them to share his.

It is this second, fuller, concept of 'fatherhood' that I am in favour of, although I also realise how difficult it is to achieve sometimes. The economic and employment situation in many countries means that jobs are getting more, not less, stressful, requiring long hours and perhaps long journeys to work as well. Therefore it may remain for many a desirable ideal rather than an achievable reality.

TEST 2, WRITING TASK 1

MODEL ANSWER

This model has been prepared by an examiner as an example of a very good answer. However, please note that this is just one example out of many possible approaches.

The chart shows the number of hours of leisure enjoyed by men and women in a typical week in 1998 – 9, according to gender and employment status.

Among those employed full-time, men on average had fifty hours of leisure, whereas women had approximately thirty-seven hours. There were no figures given for male part-time workers, but female part-timers had forty hours of leisure time, only slightly more than women in full-time employment, perhaps reflecting their work in the home.

In the unemployed and retired categories, leisure time showed an increase for both sexes, as might have been expected. Here too, men enjoyed more leisure time—over eighty hours, compared with seventy hours for women, perhaps once again reflecting the fact that women spend more time working in the home than men.

Lastly, housewives enjoyed approximately fifty-four hours of leisure, on average. There were no figures given for househusbands! Overall, the chart demonstrates that in the categories for which statistics on male leisure time were available, men enjoyed at least ten hours of extra leisure time.

TEST 2, WRETING TASK 2

MODEL ANSWER

This model has been prepared by an examiner as an example of a very good answer. However, please note that this is just one example out of many possible approaches.

Of course it goes without saying that prevention is better than cure. That is why, in recent years, there has been a growing body of opinion in favour of putting more resources into health education and preventive measures. The argument is that ignorance of , for example, basic hygiene or the dangers of an unhealthy diet or lifestyle needs to be combatted by special nationwide publicity campaigns, as well as longer-term health education.

Obviously, there is a strong human argument for catching any medical condition as early as possible. There is also an economic argument for doing so. Statistics demonstrate the cost-effectiveness of treating a condition in the early stages, rather than delaying until more expensive and prolonged treatment is necessary. Then there are social or economic costs, perhaps in terms of loss of earnings for the family concerned or unemployed benefit paid by the state.

So far so good, but the difficulties start when we try to define what the 'proportion' of the budget should be, particularly if the funds will be 'diverted from treatment'. Decisions on exactly how much of the total health budget should be spent in this way are not a matter for the non-specialist, but should be made on the basis of an accepted health service model.

This is the point at which real problems occur—the formulation of the model. How do we accurately measure which health education campaigns are effective in both medical and financial terms? How do we agree about the medical efficacy of various screening programmes, for example, when the medical establishment itself does not agree? A very rigorous process of evaluation is called for, so that we can make informed decisions.

TEST 3, WRITING TASK 1

SAMPLE ANSWER

This is an answer written by a candidate who achieved a Band 7 score. Here is the examiner's comment:

> The task is competently reported, although some details are ignored. The message is clear and there is good use of cohesive devices to organise points. Despite some minor errors in spelling and agreement, a good range of structures is used.

According to statistical information, the main reason for traveling abroad is holidays, business, and visits to friends and relatives. Indeed, there is a steady increase in the number of holiday makers; while in 1996 there were about 17,896 of the sample in 1998 there were 20,700 of them. Moreover, with the introduction of more countries within the EC market, travelling for business has also increased. Although there is not a big decrement 3,957 traveled abroad for business during 1998 compared with 3,249 in 1996. Finally, traveling abroad for visiting friends and relatives shows a steady increase over the period 1994 – 1998. While there were about 2,628 travelers in 1995 in 1998 the number increased to 3,181 in 1998. Consequently, there is a steady increase in three main reasons for travelling abroad; Holidays, business, or to visit relatives and friends.

In addition, there is also an increased change in the destinations which people tend to prefer for travelling. The area which appear to be more popular among travellers is Western Europe. Indeed, while in 1994 only 19,371 of the sample preferred to spend their holiday (or other reasons) in that main region, there was an increase to 24,519 in 1998. North America and other areas appeared also favourable. In 1996, there were 1,167 going to North America and 1,905 to other areas. These numbers increased to 1,823 and 2,486 accordingly. Statistical figures prove that Western Europe seems to be the most favourable place for holiday makers while North America and other areas follow behind.

TEST 3, WRITING TASK 2

SAMPLE ANSWER

This is an answer written by a candidate who achieved a Band 8 score. Here is the examiner's comment:

> This response is very fluent and well expressed in an appropriate register. A range of relevant issues is skilfully presented and discussed. The argument is logically developed and well organised. A wide range of structures and vocabulary are used appropriately and accurately with only minor flaws.

Before talking about the essential role of death penalty, you have to think about the meaning, and the purpose, of any kind of punishment. If you consider that the purpose is to prevent the guilty from being nasty again, you can be seduced by an argumentation in favour of the suppression of capital punishment. But you have to think about another aspect of the problem: a punishment is also useful to impress people, to make them fear the law. In fact, let's take the example of a young misfit, which has grown in a violent atmosphere, influenced by older delinquents, etc...He lives in the streets, he's got no aim but to survive. This is the kind of person who could possibly kill someone for money, or even for fun...Why would he fear prison? Life would be easier for him there. In addition, in many cases, when you behave normally, you can benefit from penalty reductions. This young misfit needs to be impressed, he needs to know that the law is a frontier. When you cross it, you can lose your life. That is why capital punishment helps keeping a distance between robbery and murder. If you abolish it, you suppress the difference between these two types of crime, which are completely different.

But there is also a limit to define: even if death penalty is unavoidable, it would be a crime to apply it to inadequate cases. If there is no premeditation or past facts which can justify such a punishment, it is far too strict to apply death penalty. That is why the lawmakers have to establish precisely the context in which capital punishment can be pronounced. That is the price to pay to limit violence without using excessive violence...

TEST 4, WRITING TASK 1

MODEL ANSWER

This model has been prepared by an examiner as an example of a very good answer. However, please note that this is just one example out of many possible approaches.

The table shows that the figures for imprisonment in the five countries mentioned indicate no overall pattern of increase of decrease. In fact there is considerable fluctuation from country to country.

In Great Britain the numbers in prison have increased steadily from 30,000 in 1930 to 80,000 in 1980. On the other hand in Australia, and particularly in New Zealand, the numbers fell markedly from 1930 to 1940. Since then they have increased gradually, apart from in 1980 when the numbers in prison in New Zealand fell by about 30,000 from the 1970 total. Canada is the only country in which the numbers in prison have decreased over the period 1930 to 1980, although there have been fluctuations in this trend. The figures for the United States indicate the greatest number of prisoners compared to the other four countries but population size needs to be taken into account in this analysis. The prison population in the United States increased rapidly from 1970 to 1980 and this must be a worrying trend.

TEST 4, WRITING TASK 2

MODEL ANSWER

This model has been prepared by an examiner as an example of a very good answer. However, please note that this is just one example out of many possible approaches.

It is certainly true that the position of women in society has undergone a dramatic change in the past twenty years but I do not feel that this is a direct cause of the indisputable increase in juvenile-related problems during this period.

It is now accepted that young women should find work on leaving school; indeed to rely totally on their parents' financial support is no longer an option in many families. Likewise, once they get married, the majority of women continue working since the financial pressures of setting up a house and establishing a reasonable standard of living often require two incomes.

Twenty years ago it was common for women to give up work once they had children and devote their time to caring for their children. This is no longer the general rule and the provision of professionally-run child care facilities and day nurseries have removed much of the responsibility for child rearing that used to fall to mothers. However, these facilities come at a cost and often require two salaries coming into a family to be afforded.

I do not believe that the increase in the number of working mothers has resulted in children being brought up less well than previously. Indeed it could be argued that by giving mothers the opportunity to work and earn extra money children can be better provided for than previously. There is more money for luxuries and holidays and a more secure family life is possible. Of course there are limits as to the amount of time that ideally should be spent away from home and the ideal scenario would be for one of the parents (often the wife) to have a part-time job and thus be available for their children before and after school. It is important to establish the correct balance between family life and working life.

TEST A WRITING TASK 1 (GENERAL TRAINING)

MODEL ANSWER

This model has been prepared by an examiner as an example of a very good answer. However, please note that this is just one example out of many possible approaches.

Dear Sir or Madam,

I an writing this letter to explain why I have been unable to return the three books I have out on three-day loan, which are now overdue. After taking the books out on 16th March, I had an urgent phone call from my elderly aunt's neighbour to say that my aunt had had a fall and had been taken into hospital. I am her only surviving relative in this country, so I felt I had to go and see her immediately. I travelled down to Surrey the following morning, thinking I would stay for only two or three days. Unfortunately, my aunt's condition has only improved very slowly, so I have had to stay here longer than expected. However, the hospital says that if all goes well, she should be able to go home in two or three days' time, in which case I will be back at the beginning of next week.

Bearing in mind the circumstances, I trust you will kindly waive any fines that may have accumulated.

Yours sincerely,

TEST A WRITING TASK 2 (GENERAL TRAINING)

MODEL ANSWER

This model has been prepared by an examiner as an example of a very good answer. However, please note that this is just one example out of many possible approaches.

It is certainly very understandable that some governments should start looking at ways of limiting their populations to a sustainable figure. In the past, populations were partly regulated by frequent war and widespread disease, but in recent years the effects of those factors have been diminished. Countries can be faced with a population that is growing much faster than the nation's food resources or employment opportunities and whose members can be condemned to poverty by the need to feed extra mouths. They identify population control as a means to raising living standards.

But how should it be achieved? Clearly, this whole area is a very delicate personal and cultural issue. Many people feel that this is not a matter for the state. They feel this is one area of life where they have the right to make decisions for themselves. For that reason, it would seem that the best approach would be to work by persuasion rather than compulsion. This could be done by a process of education that points out the way a smaller family can mean an improved quality of life for the family members, as will as less strain on the country's, perhaps very limited, resources.

This is the preferred way. Of course, if this does not succeed within a reasonable time scale, it may be necessary to consider other measures, such as tax incentives or child-benefit payments for small families only. These are midway between persuasion and compulsion.

So, yes, it is sometimes necessary, but governments should try very hard to persuade first. They should also remember that this is a very delicate area indeed, and that social engineering can create as many problems as it solves.

TEST B WRITING TASK 1 (GENERAL TRAINING)

SAMPLE ANSWER

This is an answer written by a candidate who achieved a Band 7 score. Here is the examiner's comment:

> The response is relevant and fairly fluent, although some aspects of the task could be more fully developed. The message is well organised and can be followed throughout. A fairly good range of vocabulary and structure is used, although occasional spelling errors and faulty word choice detract slightly from the overall fluency.

Dear Sirs,

I was one of the passengers who took the flight from Narita (Tokyo) to Heathrow (London) on 5 August. Unfortunately, my suitcase did not come out after the flight. Although I have explained this Mr. McDonald who was in charge at the Luggage Claim Office I have not heard from him as of now.

My suit case is grey Samsonite whose size is 70×95cm. There are 3 steckers on one side and 1 heart shaped stecker on the other side. My initials "AR" are also written on both sides.

There are a few books and a copy of my thesis in that suitcase, which I need for the conference on 19 August.

So I would deeply appreciate it if you could give me a prompt reply at your most convenient. My flight number, luggage claim number and address are written below.

> *Flight No: NH 201*
> *Luggage Claim No: 00026*
> *Address: 64 Silver Street*
> *London. NW165AL*

Yours Faithfully,

TEST B WRITING TASK 2 (GENERAL TRAINING)

SAMPLE ANSWER

This is an answer written by a candidate who achieved a Band 6 score. Here is the examiner's comment:

> This response is underlength and is marked down because of this. Only a few relevant ideas are presented and these are used rather repetitively and are insufficiently developed or supported. However, the writing communicates fluently and a satisfactory range of structures and vocabulary are used.

I am not surprise when I read in the newspapers that many people move to English speaking countries. I am an engineer in a process control since ten years and I understand the necessity of English language. For example, when I read technical English specifications, when I meet Japanese industrials to build together some electronic materials or when I go on holidays in Italy where the best way (for me) to communicate is to speak English. Therefore, today, it's necessary to learn English and the best way is to study in English as soon as possible when we are at school but also when we have a job. It's so important to communicate with foreigners, because of work. For example: to sell foods in USA, to build electronic cards with the Japanese, to obtain a certification with FDA (American organization) in order to sell some pharmaceutical products. In fact, it's important for everybody: the workers, the visitors, the scientists, etc...

These are the main reason which explain why so many people go to English speaking countries (the best way to learn) and why English is such an important international language (the communication between many the people over the world).

Sample Answer Sheet

 University of Cambridge
Local Examinations Syndicate
International Examinations

 The British Council

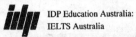 IDP Education Australia:
IELTS Australia

Centre number:

Please write your **name** below,

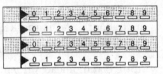

then write your four digit **Candidate** number in the boxes and
shade the number in the grid on the right.

Test date:

Day: 1 2 3 4 5 6 7 8 9 10 11 12 13 14 15 16 17 18 19 20 21 22 23 24 25 26 27 28 29 30 31

Month: 1 2 3 4 5 6 7 8 9 10 11 12   Last digit of the **Year:** 0 1 2 3 4 5 6 7 8 9

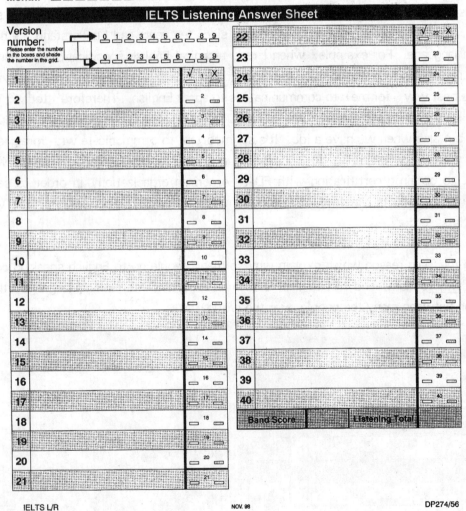

IELTS L/R   NOV. 98   DP274/56

IELTS Reading Answer Sheet

Module taken:

Academic ▭   General Training ▭

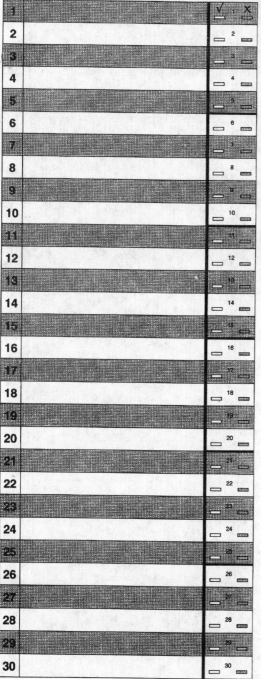

1		✓	X
2		2	
3		3	
4		4	
5		5	
6		6	
7		7	
8		8	
9		9	
10		10	
11		11	
12		12	
13		13	
14		14	
15		15	
16		16	
17		17	
18		18	
19		19	
20		20	
21		21	
22		22	
23		23	
24		24	
25		25	
26		26	
27		27	
28		28	
29		29	
30		30	

31		✓	X
32		32	
33		33	
34		34	
35		35	
36		36	
37		37	
38		38	
39		39	
40		40	

| Band Score | | Reading Total | |